WHITE'S TAVERN

Jim Altfeld

A T Publishing
23 Lily Lake Road
Highland, NY 12528

Copyright © 2021 Jim Altfeld.

All rights reserved. No part of this publication may be reproduced, distributed, or transmitted in any form or by any means, including photocopying, recording, or other electronic or mechanical methods, without the prior written permission of the publisher, except in the case of brief quotations embodied in critical reviews and certain other noncommercial uses permitted by copyright law. For permission requests, write to the publisher, addressed
"Attention: Permissions Coordinator," at the address below.

ISBN: 978-0-9740534-9-3

Book design by David Schneider.

First printing edition 2021.

A T Publishing
23 Lily Lake Road
Highland, NY 12528

Disclaimer

White's Tavern is a work of fiction. The stories and characters are fictitious. Certain long-standing institutions, agencies, and public offices are mentioned, but the characters involved, at least for the most part, are wholly imaginary. Any resemblance to actual events or persons, living or dead, is entirely coincidental, with the exception of the Chicago Outfit and White's Tavern, which were very real. An enormous <u>Thank You</u> to the many real-life characters portrayed in this book for accepting me as one of their own. The book is truly fictitious and not intended to hurt anyone, living or dead. Should that be the case, I regret any unintentional harm resulting from the publishing and marketing of White's Tavern.

Dedication

First and foremost, this book is dedicated to the two most influential and highly inspirational people in my life – my late parents. Both possessed a great sense of humor coupled with a generosity of spirit and an insatiable hunger to learn, grow, and experience life right up to the time they died... all of which left an indelible imprint on their impressionable son. They were truly the greatest role models any son could have.

In addition to my parents, I owe much to my older brother George who forced me to learn how to deal with complex, complicated, screwed up and extremely straightforward people, all of which he was. Two tours in Nam and being awarded two bronze stars and two purple hearts tells you much about his character, but doesn't explain all that went on in that brilliant mind of his. I feel fortunate to have had him as a brother. Have to add that the two funniest people I have ever encountered in my life are Bill Ott and my brother. Bill had a wet sense of humor and extremely quick wit, while my brother's was extremely dry.

Finally, I dedicate this book to William Robert Ott, without whom this book may have never seen the light of day. Bill was charming, highly intelligent, tough, full goose Bozo nuts, fun, spontaneous, athletic, an alcoholic, and an unforgettable character like none other. Bill and I were exceptionally close and cared for one another as only two guys who'd known one another since age six could.

Thank you, Schatz and Joe, George, and Bill for being in my life.

• CHAPTER ONE •

His first arrest came in 1966 at age 17.

"Rack 'em."

"Fuck you, I'll rack 'em"

The game was eight ball. The year was 1966 and a buck went a long way. Twenty went even further.

"Twenty says you don't make the shot."

"You even got twenty?"

"Right here, jagoff." showing the Jefferson.

Bill Ott, quick, wide, muscular, athletic and an inch shy of six feet, lined up the angle of his shot, cigarette dangling from his lip. He glanced over, nodded and approved the bet.

"Ok, asshole, you're on."

Relaxing his intense position, Bill stood straight up and approached his opponent. "Tell you what. Let's double the bet."

"Fuck you, we're stickin' with the $20."

Bill strode back to his place at the table, chalked his cue and leaned over the green felt table. His eyes were wide and fixed as he sized up the angle to make the shot. Slowly, ever so slowly, he pumped the cue stick between his fingers bridged upon the hard slate table. He got his rhythm. Silence filled the room. Nerves pumped sweat through open pores.

"Hey, who owns the four-door green Buick out front?!?"

Every head turned but Bill's. A small bead of perspiration appeared on Bill's upper lip, but he never moved a muscle. Didn't even twitch.

In the doorway stood a part-time rookie cop.

"Hey, you fuckin' degenerates, I asked ya who owns the fuckin Buick and I want a fuckin answer!"

Still holding his position, keeping his eye on the cue ball with a myopic squint, Bill answered, "I do."

"Well, move it Jack, you're blockin' the goddamn driveway."

"I'm busy." Bill's eyes were welded on the cue ball.

"What did you just say, punk?" the cop asked briskly approaching Bill.

"I said, I'd move it after I make this fuckin shot." Bill felt the cop get closer.

"No, punk. I don't think you understand me. Move that goddamn car and move it now."

Bill remained silent and motionless holding his ground, but his face had changed, like an eerie sky just before the thunder clapped. The cop grabbed Bill's well-developed arm. The cue stick moved and the balls scattered across the table. Bill snapped.

It was quick as no one spoke. In one sweeping motion, Bill had lifted the cop off his feet and threw him on the table like a load of wet plaster. Knuckles pounded flesh as the rookie cop's nose went bust. Bone showed through. Two teeth splintered with the second punch. The green felt grew dark as it absorbed the blood. Bill spent the next two weeks in jail. His mother had some difficulty coming up with the $1000.00 bail money on a $10,000.00 bond.

But it didn't really start there for Bill. Early on he showed a real talent for shoplifting. As a matter of fact, Bill could go through a corner grocery store and come out with six packages of Twinkies, a Dunkin Yo-Yo and a gallon of milk, never having paid for any of it. Even more than shoplifting, he loved to fight. As an only child, his mom seemed to spend more time in the local grade school than Bill did, pleading with Mr. Patterson, the school's principal to not expel her only son.

"But, Mrs. Ott, Bill could have seriously injured the Colotto kid with that brick."

"He's just hyperactive like all kids are." she'd cry.

"But, Mrs. Ott, Bill was caught stealing Twinkies from Larsen's store, again."

"You know he's really smart and probably just bored. You tested him yourself. He's got an IQ of 154!!" she'd retort.

"But, Mrs. Ott, Bill ripped the top of his school desk right off the hinges."

"I'll pay for it."

"But, Mrs. Ott, Bill caused over $300.00 worth of damage to the bathroom with that cherry bomb."

"But he writes such beautiful poetry!"

"But, Mrs. Ott..."

Each time she would bail her Billy out refusing to accept the fact that there was a germ of destruction in him. Truth be known, her precious, wonderful son was neither precious nor wonderful. Fortunately, Bill didn't kill things...he only destroyed them.

"The happiest day is that day in the past that you can always run back to when you find the present to be just too unbearable." Author Anon

• CHAPTER TWO •

"Whiskey!! Goddamn it, I want whiskey!"

"Quit watchin' those fuckin Bonanza re-runs and shut the fuck up already!"

A spilled rum and coke scurried down the bar as the first face of the evening slowly plunged into the sticky brew.

"Would somebody get DT outta here?!?"

Hot steamy air blew in through two screen doors, bringing with it absolutely no comfort, only more heat. It was another typical, hot, sticky, humid July night in Chicago. Grand Avenue ran east and west right through River Grove and Elmwood Park, two Western Suburbs located about 12 miles West of Chicago's Loop. River Grove was roughly 2600 North and 8600 West with the corner of State and Madison in Chicago being the East/West and North/South axis points respectively. In other words, Grand Avenue in River Grove was 26 blocks north of Madison and eighty-six blocks west of State. The primary business district in River Grove was Grand and Thatcher. Just two blocks east of that, on the northeast corner stood White's Tavern where whiskey confessions and therapy sessions abound. It was a place that provided roots. The kind of roots that reached down and dug deep, grabbing the ground with such force that not only could you not break its grip, you really didn't want to.

Old man White built the tavern back in the 1950s when lunch cost 95 cents and you drank until the bartender asked you how many you had at 25 cents a pop. It was a place where men could be men and do whatever the hell they wanted. All wood and the floors slanted so badly someone would occasionally roll a green cats-eye marble across it. Outside, there's a front and back stoop each with three wooden steps that weren't exactly straight. The roof was flat with a rickety rusted iron ladder that was the only way up there. It's the same one a burglar used to climb in hopes of breaking into White's, but broke both arms and his collarbone when he fell off on the way down. But that's another story. All told, White's was a rectangular, dirty grey, two story building with square rotting windows and two broken screen doors that did little to keep the flies out. Some felt the paint was peeling, but it seemed more like it was just shedding. For sure, it was neither quaint, nor picturesque... it was just worn out, old and sagging. There was little doubt that White's was badly in need of repairs and improvements, none of which Earl the owner was going to spring for. The second story was a dingy flat that absorbed much of the noise, music and smells coming from the tavern below. The flat was also where Earl and his wife Marge resided.

Inside the tavern, the bar took up about a third of the space while the area for the puck sliding bowling game took up a little less than a quarter. The four booths that ran along the front window were of red vinyl that hadn't been reupholstered since the Hoover Administration. Oh, and the sawdust. Earl made a point to have just enough sawdust on the floor to sop up the spilled booze, blood, broken teeth, or whatever it was that needed sopping up. He never seemed to have enough sawdust to sop up Mitchell Sorensen or D.T, who had about as much get up and go between them as a floor mop. Both were notorious for drinking themselves into unconsciousness, sliding off their bar stools and landing on the floor where they would remain the rest of the night. It didn't matter that someone else would be occupying the stool with one or both of them underneath it. They were fine where they were.

River Grove itself was a typical northwest suburb, part of Leyden Township, full of hard working, hard drinking, blue collar people living in small, blue collar homes. But what River Grove and the other suburbs all had in common was the Chicago Outfit.

For example, on Friday, June 14, 1957 when my friends and I were all about eight years old, the following story appeared in the Chicago Daily Tribune. Just under the headline there was a picture of guy named Argentine who looked the worst for wear and a caption to go with it.

Two Federal Agents Wounded in Narcotic Ring Gun Battle

With his undershirt soaked in blood and wearing two black eyes, a man identified as Dominic Argentine, 38, owner of the Triangle Inn is escorted into a Chicago police station. Two federal narcotics agents and a suspected dope peddler were wounded in a wild gun battle at the tavern, yesterday.

Two federal agents, one a Hammond man and a man described as a dope gang gunman were critically wounded early today in a shooting spree that began in a River Grove, Ill tavern.

John Ripa, 32 of Hammond was reported recovering this noon after four and one-half hours on the operating table in Oak Park Hospital. Doctors removed a bullet in his back and reported he "has a good chance of recovering."

His partner in the dope-busters, Jack E. Love, 31 of Chicago, was reported in poor condition with a bullet still in him, just above the heart. Both agents are married and have children.

Carlos (Bananas) Urbinatti, 40, named as the gunman for the narcotics gang, was reported "in very bad shape" with a bullet in his head.

The three were wounded at the Triangle Inn. 1st Avenue and Thatcher Road, River Grove after Ripa and another agent, Ralph Eckhardt, went into the tavern to follow up on a dope purchase from Tony Matas, a suspected peddler, by a third agent.

U.S. District Attorney John Grady said in court hours later that the agents had walked into a trap "set by a ruthless gang of wholesale dope peddlers who had learned the identity of the agents."

Albert E. Aman, district supervisor of the narcotics bureau gave this account of the shooting.

"Agents Ripa and Eckhardt, following weeks of investigation, made a buy of $3,000 worth of heroin from a ring member named Tommy Matas in Chicago's Loop yesterday afternoon. They were to pick up the narcotics early today at the Triangle Inn."

Aman continued, "Ripa and Eckhardt entered the tavern shortly after midnight and mingled with customers for about 40 minutes, eating sandwiches and acting as customers, and waiting for the drug delivery, when Dominic Argentine, 38, co-owner of the tavern shot Ripa in the back without warning. Eckhardt then dragged his partner outside where four other narcotics men were waiting and alerted the men of trouble.

Just then" Aman went on to say, "Urbinatti, 40, the trigger man and a patron of the tavern earlier, drove into the parking lot and shot agent Jack E. Love, 37, who was among the covering agents immediately encircling the gunman's car. Another agent then shot Urbinatti in the head, arms and shoulder as he tried to shoot his way through four agents surrounding his automobile."

River Grove Police Chief Robert O'Hallen, receiving a shooting report, radioed for help from any police in the area.

Four squads of state police, four of Cook County and two each from River Grove and Elmwood Park, Franklin Park and one each from Schiller Park and Norridge Park responded. In the belief that Dominic Argentine was still inside, about 50 federal agents, and state, county, and suburban police riddled the Triangle Inn roadhouse for 45 minutes filling the building with tear gas from 20 shells and at least 25 rounds of machine gun ammunition.

When they finally entered, two hours later, police found the tavern empty. They later arrested Argentine at his home.

Also arrested as members of the gang, were Joseph Bruno (alias Gardini) 45, said to be a major narcotics wholesaler in Chicago and Matas, 33, described as a peddler.

Argentine's brother and partner, Steve, was questioned by River Grove police but was released several hours later.

Aman said Urbinatti had $500 of marked bills in his pocket, adding the money had been used by undercover agents to purchase narcotics from Matas.

He said the buy from Matas was to have been the last one in a series being made to "wrap up" the case against the gang.

The supervisor said the gang used the Triangle Inn as a hangout.

Bruno was questioned by Senator Daniel (D-Texas) in the Senate judiciary subcommittee probe of nationwide dope racketeering.

Bruno was cited for contempt of Congress after he refused 78 times to answer questions pleading Fifth Amendment protection.

On March 29, a contempt indictment with six counts was returned against him by the federal grand jury in Chicago.

The best part of the story for those of us who lived in River Grove was that the Triangle Inn was located less than a block away from the police station. The worst part of the story is that Bill Ott's parents lived directly across from the Triangle Inn causing Bill and his family to be evacuated due to the tear gas floating into their home.

Then a mere four-years later, in 1961, River Grove experienced yet more excitement when this headline appeared on September 9th of that year.

Chicago Daily Tribune, September 9, 1961
Police Find $37,000 in Gangster's Flat

Police Hunt Him in Pinball Beating Case

Jury Names 3 Suburb Cops

State's attorney's police seized $37,000 in cash and gambling records and devices yesterday in the home of Sam (Big Sam) Ariola, a crime syndicate gangster, shortly after he and five others, including three River Grove policemen, reportedly were named in true bills in the baseball bat beating of two pinball machine gamblers.

Outside the building, detectives found Ariola's car which contained a loaded pistol, a tear gas gun, and hundreds of matchbook lottery tickets which are peddled through county saloons by the crime syndicate.

Police said Ariola's flat was crammed with betting records and gambling devices, including horoscope gambling machines, jar game equipment and lottery tickets.

Bank records and other documents apparently relating to mysterious financial transactions by Ariola also were found in the apartment. In a bookcase, detectives said they found a special police badge issued by the police department of Franklin Park.

The betting records, Spencer said, covered the operations of Ariola's large handbooks and pinball games in Franklin Park and River Grove from April to July, 1960.

The cash, betting records, gambling devices, and papers which listed Ariola's big money deals were confiscated by detectives and taken to the state's attorney's office.

Spencer's investigators began an effort to trace Ariola's dealings through a bank in Du Page county. Stubs for checks from the bank, Spencer said, showed a $2,500 payment from Ariola to River Grove Fire Chief Schmidt.

Other check stubs revealed that Ariola made a $10,500 payment to Carl Colletti on October 22, 1958 and paid $10,540 to Harold Arado last April 13.

Chief Schmidt admitted to The Tribune last night that he had received the money from Ariola four years ago during the construction of a $125,000 apartment building at River Grove

Avenue and Thatcher Road. Fire Chief Schmidt said the building had been financed by his construction company, Ariola and Ariola's sister.

According to Schmidt, "Ariola gave me the $2,500 when his sister couldn't come up with her share of the money. Later on, when the building was completed, I sold out my interest in the project."

Schmidt said he had known Ariola for a decade as a pinball machine and juke box operator. The gangster's pinball games are operating now, Schmidt said, in a tavern in a River Grove bowling alley owned by Schmidt. He claimed however, that he leased the drinking place to another man who brought in the Ariola gambling games.

Arado, 47, owner of an Oak Park dry cleaning shop, told The Tribune last night that he had received the $10,500 in a cashier's check bearing the name of Ariola as a payment on Mannheim road property that he sold to a "motel syndicate" in 1957. Arado said he expected to receive the final payment next year on the purchase price of $38,500.

The hoard of currency, most of it in $500 and $100 bills, was discovered by detectives led by Roswell T. Spencer, the state's attorney's chief investigator, in Ariola's five room apartment over his gambling headquarters at 9757 Franklin Street, Franklin Park. The currency had been stuffed in a briefcase.

Ariola apparently harvested the cash, Spencer said, from the horse parlors and pinball games he supervises for the crime syndicate in Franklin Park and River Grove.

In those two suburbs, Ariola is "muscle" man and collector for three syndicate chiefs – John (Jackie the Lackey) Cerone, Sam (Teetz) Battaglia, and Joseph (Joe Gags) Gagliano.

The raid on Ariola's hideaway, where police found an exercise machine used by the gangster to build up his arm muscles, resulted in the disclosure that Ariola and his kinfolk had set up a building construction partnership four years ago with Fire Chief Henry J. Schmidt of River Grove.

Ariola was not in the apartment when police arrived. He is still being sought.

To provide further background on how well entrenched the mob was in the Elmwood Park, River Grove, and the adjoining suburbs, Jackie Cerone lived at 2000 N. 77th Avenue in Elmwood Park. Cerone was highly trusted by Accardo, Ricca and DeBiase. He began as a driver for Accardo and then became a protégé of Giancana. To say the man was a sick, greatly feared, psychopathic fuck was putting it mildly. Cerone also controlled a swathe of the West Side from the Chicago River west to Harlem Avenue and north of the Eisenhower Expressway. Cerone was also a protégé of Accardo and Ricca and became big in the 60s. He eventually became the top boss in 1967 when Sam Battaglia, Sr. went to prison. But two years later, Cerone and five others were in prison, thanks to the testimony of a small-time bookie named Louis "Lou" Bombacino. The problem was that without a doubt, Cerone was one of the most feared and volatile people on the planet. The Outfit finally caught up with Bombacino years later in Tempe, Arizona in October of 1975 for having snitched and finished him off with a car bomb using military grade plastique. As for Salvator "teets" Battaglia, he lived in Oak Park and was close to both Giancana and Ricca. He was later appointed as Boss over the West Side's gambling and prostitution interests. Finally, but far more complicated is Joseph (Joe Gags) Gagliano. In 1961, John DiFronzo, age 35, was nabbed in Stone Park for hijacking a tractor-trailer full of cigarettes. He was a resident of Seventy-Third Avenue in the village of Elmwood Park, found to be the lead collector and enforcer of the gang. Joseph "Joe Gags" Gagliano, forty-nine, of 1731 Thatcher Road in Elmwood Park, was believed to be its chief. Joseph "Joey the Clown" Lombardo, thirty-three, was a member. Investigators learned that the gang met March 9, 1961, with William "Willie Potatoes" Daddano, supervisor of Outfit rackets in Kane, DuPage and McHenry Counties. Daddano suggested that they expand their influence by channeling loansharking profits into legitimate businesses. The gang then met August 4, 1961, with Daddano and "Mad Sam" DeStefano. DeStefano led his own gang of Outfit loan sharks in northwest Chicago. Charges were brought against the gang members in December 1963. John DiFronzo was accused of being one of those who kidnaped, threatened and tortured a factory worker named Weisphal. Gagliano's group was unruly at arraignment. They refused to cooperate in their processing. They would not be fingerprinted. They even distorted their faces in front of the photographer. They only relented when criminal court judges refused to consider release on bail until proper processing had taken place. Six defendants were brought to trial in March of 1964 for the kidnapping and beating of Weisphal. They were Joseph Gagliano, John DiFronzo, Joseph Lombardo, William "Wee Willie" Messino, and two former policeman, Albert A. Sarno and Chris Cardi. A mistrial was declared in early April, as authorities investigated an apparent attempt by a former police officer to bribe a juror. Then in May, the case was brought back into court. Joseph Lombardo was released because Weisphal could not identify him as one of the men who beat him. Weisphal told the jury that he was taken against his will to the basement of a tavern in Elmwood Park and handcuffed to a ceiling pipe. Gang members then beat and kicked him. The jury found Weisphal an unconvincing witness and had trouble with some inconsistencies in the prosecution's case. After a trial of seven days, the jury deliberated for three and a half hours before deciding to acquit the five remaining defendants.

So, as you see, the Outfit was not only well ensconced in the village of River Grove as well as all the neighboring suburbs, but there certainly were a lot of players within the mob. Now, getting back to the Tribune reporting on the "baseball bat beating", that story was followed the next day by:

Chicago Daily Tribune, September 10, 1961
PROSECUTOR RIPS MOVE BY CHIEF IN RIVER GROVE

A controversy flared last night between the state's attorney's office and the River Grove police department over the beating case in which three of the suburb's policemen have been accused of conspiring with crime syndicate gangsters.

Bitter words flew between Edward Egan, first assistant state's attorney and Police Chief Robert O'Hallen of River Grove, after O'Hallen obtained warrants for the arrest of the bludgeoning victims, who now are under police guard.

The victims, Melvin Raymond Kent, 28, a 300-pound short order cook and Peter Gothard, 28, a salesman, admitted that they had manipulated a pinball machine with a wire to gain a $72.00 payoff.

Afterward, the charged River Grove policemen seized them and turned them over to three gangsters, who took them to a warehouse and beat them with baseball bats.

O'Hallen insisted that his men were innocent and that the "whole case is a frameup." He went on to say, "My men are good men and I trust them." He also admitted that pinball machines had been operating in Al's Grill at 8322 Grand Avenue, River Grove where Kent and Gothard said they were seized by police, and in other saloons and bowling alleys in the suburb.

The county grand jury charged three River Grove policemen, Lt. Robert Tobin, and Patrolmen Roland W. Letcher and Herman Bingham with malfeasance and conspiracy. The gangsters are Sam "Big Sam" Ariola, the crime syndicate's gambling supervisor in River Grove and Franklin Park and his henchmen, Louis Epoli, 28 and Guy (Chuck) Cervone, 22.

Also arrested was Larry Russell, 23, of 2514 Erie St., in River Grove of gambling charges. Russell was the counter man in Al's Grill, 8334 Grand Avenue, River Grove, where Gothard and Kent obtained the pinball payoff. Russell admitted that he split the payoff with them.

Russell was booked on gambling charges and released on $200 bond for appearance before the court on September 1st.

Three days later that story was followed by:

Chicago Tribune, September 13, 1961
Gambler, Pal Surrender in Gang Beating

Two hoodlums surrendered yesterday in connection with the baseball bat beating of two pinball cheats, while a third reportedly admitted to state's attorney's police that the story told by the victims was true.

Sam (Big Sam) Ariola, 37, and Louis Epoli, 28, of 818 N. 23rd Avenue, Melrose Park walked into the state's attorney's office with their attorney, George Bieber, but refused to say anything about the case.

Their companion, Guy (Chuck) Cervone, 22, of 123 N. 22nd Avenue, Melrose Park refused to sign a statement, although it was reported that he admitted orally to brutal treatment of two men allegedly surrendered to the hoodlums by River Grove police.

Ariola and Epoli were released in $5,000 bond for appearance September 22, before M.J. Berkos, justice of the peace in Riverside, on charges of assault with intent to commit mayhem. Cervone, who was arrested last week, is scheduled to appear Friday in justice of the peace court in Lyons.

All three men reportedly have been named by the grand jury in a true bill charging conspiracy to commit aggravated assault.

Three River Grove policemen, Lt. Robert Tobin and Patrolmen Roland W. Letcher and Herman Bingham reportedly have been named by the grand jury in true bills charging conspiracy and malfeasance in office.

Roswell T. Spencer, chief investigator for the state's attorney's office, indicated that a little gray book containing the names and phone numbers of politicians, policemen, union chiefs and hoodlums found in Ariola's headquarters in Franklin Park last week, might be turned over to the Federal Bureau of Investigation.

"The names do not appear to have any connection with our present investigation," Spencer said.

Ariola, Epoli and Cervone are charged with the beating on September 1, of Melvin R. Kent, 28, a short order cook of 3110 W. 67th Street, Maywood and Peter Gothard, 28 a salesman, of 319 W. 67th Avenue, Maywood, after Kent and Gothard had used a piece of wire to trip the mechanism of a pinball machine for a $72 payoff in a River Grove restaurant.

According to Kent, he and Gothard were seized by Letcher and Bingham, September 1 and were accompanied by Ariola who slugged him once before being placed in a police patrol car and driven to the River Grove Police Station. There, Kent related that he and Gothard were turned over to Ariola, Cervone and Epoli by officers Tobin, Letcher and Bingham. From there they were placed in another car and told by Officer Bingham, "You don't need to worry about coming back, you won't be able to walk."

The three gangsters, Kent and Gothard then drove to a warehouse at 3340 Lincoln Avenue, Franklin Park. Ariola held them under a gun in the warehouse, they said, while Cervone and Epoli beat them with baseball bats.

The beatings continued, the victims said, until the bats were broken.

Kent, it was related, suffered a broken left arm and several broken ribs, and Gothard's body was a mass of bruises. They said they then were driven back to their car in River Grove. They said Ariola released them with a warning that they would be killed if they told police about the beating.

Last week, however, Kent ignored the alleged death threat and reported the assault to the state's attorney's office, which opened the grand jury investigation.

Police Chief Robert O'Hallen of River Grove, who has defended the three policemen against charges by Kent and Gothard that the officers surrendered the men to the hoodlums the night of September 1 in the village police station, appeared before the grand jury yesterday for a second time.

William J. Post of 8514 River Grove Avenue, River Grove, a reserve policeman identified by Kent as the fourth man in the police station the night of September 1 when the hoodlums took custody of Kent and Gothard, also appeared before the grand jury. He reportedly told the *grand jury he was in the station that night but was not present at the time Kent claims that he was.*

Spencer confirmed reports that Gothard had vanished, but said he believed Gothard was there.

To set the stage further and provide additional history, it needs to be said that the Chicago Outfit began long before 1957. It also needs to be known that one of the original leading players was Roger "The Terrible" Touhy. Touhy was an Irish American mob boss and prohibition-era bootlegger from Chicago. He is best remembered for having been framed for the 1933 faked kidnapping of gangster John "Jake the Barber" Factor, a brother of cosmetics manufacturer Max Factor, Sr.

Touhy partnered with Matt Kolb, who was already supplying the Chicago Outfit with a third of its beer and running highly profitable gambling and loan sharking operations north of Chicago.

The two men established a brewery and cooperate, which made barrels and casks. Producing high-quality beer, they were soon selling 1,000 barrels a week at $55 a barrel, a profit of over 90%. In 1926, Touhy expanded into illegal gambling and installed slot machines in speakeasies throughout the northwest Chicago suburbs, which grossed over $1 million in the first year. Johnny Touhy was killed at the Lone Tree Inn, near Niles, just north of Chicago, in December 1927 allegedly by gunmen belonging to gangster Al Capone's Chicago Outfit.

By 1929, Al Capone was ordering hundreds of barrels of beer a week from Roger Touhy, but he soon became envious of Touhy and Kolb's operations and wanted to take over the profitable business. Capone began to send thugs to Touhy's headquarters, to talk his way into a partnership, but Touhy refused.

Capone then began to push into Touhy's territory, opening whorehouses just inside Des Plains and sending in beer salesmen who drastically undercut Touhy's prices. Roger and his brothers pushed back and warned any saloon keeper who sold Capone's beer inside their territory would be busted up. When Joseph Touhy and his crew were busting up a speakeasy that Capone had opened in Schiller Park, Joseph was shot dead in June of 1929.

Capone continued to pressure Roger Touhy to hand over control of his operations, but Touhy resisted. In 1931, Roger approached local law enforcement officers and others to ask for their support, explaining that all he wanted to do was sell beer. In contrast, Capone and his men would bring lawlessness, gambling, and prostitution to the area. Local leaders agreed to help him and refused to buy Capone's low-quality beer or utilize his gambling products. In response, Capone ordered Matt Kolb killed in October 1931.

Afterward, all-out war broke out between the Touhy Gang and the Chicago Outfit, with sporadic gun battles occurring in rural Cook County over the next few years. In the meantime, Capone and his men were pushing against Chicago's labor unions, who soon decided to band together for protection and pitched into a $75,000 fund that was handed over to Tommy Touhy. Roger Touhy also won the support of Chicago Mayor Anton Cermak, who promised police department protection for his gang if they helped win the war against the syndicate. The war between the two gangster factions then spread into the Chicago city limits. According to the *Chicago Tribune*, in 1932, nearly 100 gangsters were killed.

By the spring of 1933, it appeared that the Touhy Gang was winning the war against the syndicate. Then the mob killed Mayor Anton Cermak in front of visiting President, Franklin D. Roosevelt and shot Tommy Touhy, though he survived and was later imprisoned. Later, the union bosses in Chicago surrendered to the mob. Possibly the greatest theatrical act of all time by any politician occurred when the dying Mayor Cermak looked at FDR and said, *"Better me than you, Mr. President."* Cermak had no doubt who had shot him.

The end of Roger Touhy's reign came when he and two of his henchmen were convicted in state court at Chicago on February 23, 1934, and sentenced to serve 99 years in prison for kidnapping John "Jake the Barber" Factor and holding him for ransom. Roger Touhy was quickly forgotten about after he was received in the Statesville Penitentiary at Joliet, Illinois, in 1934. It wasn't long before he escaped Joliet, but was caught and returned.

Then on July 31, 1957, the Illinois governor commuted Touhy's original 99-year sentence to 72 years and reduced his 199-year sentence for escaping to three years. Touhy subsequently won parole for the kidnapping. Under the parole terms, he had to serve six more months for the kidnapping and the full three-year sentence for the escape. On November 13, 1959, Touhy was granted parole and left prison on November 24, 1959 – 25 years and nine months after his incarceration.

Just 22 days after his prison release, Roger Touhy and his bodyguard were gunned down by a mob hit men on December 16, 1959. A reminder to all that the Outfit never forgets and there are no expiration dates on a Contract.

The Touhy brothers may have disappeared but the Outfit most certainly did not. When prohibition ended in 1933, the mob looked for a new source of income and found it in the trade unions which they began taking over. Funny when you think about the fact that they were the first to use Vertical Integration or Roll Ups long before it became common place in business. What the mob clearly understood was that if you control the union, you then control the workforce. And if you can control the workforce, you automatically control the industry that the workforce works in and can put a stranglehold on it.

Another thing the mob saw was people running to the suburbs and fleeing the city. So, taking advantage of this observation, they began taking over suburban towns like Elmwood Park, River Grove, Schiller Park, Franklin Park, Melrose Park, Bellwood, Northlake, Rosemont, Stone Park, Maywood, Oak Park, River Forest, Norridge Park, and Lombard to name a few. Part of their taking over included buying up single family homes in these towns and specifically homes that had basements, in order to turn the homes into makeshift casinos. Plus, there were establishments like Casa Madrid in Melrose Park on 25th Street, just south of Lake Street and the DB Lounge also on 25th but south of North Avenue, that were well known for gambling. In addition, there were a great many wonderful, mob owned suburban restaurants like Slicker Sam's, The Come Back Inn, Tom's Steak House, Horwath's, Gene & Georgetti's, the Leather Bottle, the Boar's Head, The Carlisle, Beyond Meo's, Rocky's, Auroi's, and the York Pub to name but a few of the better ones.

The suburbs were controlled out of River Forest by Tony Accardo, alias Joe Batters or The Big Tuna. Anthony Joseph Accardo was a one-time Capone bodyguard and hitman who was thought to have participated in the St. Valentine's Day Massacre. Mr. Accardo lived at 915 Franklin Street in River Forest where he ruled Chicago for some 60 years. But, above Mr. Accardo was Paul "the Waiter" Ricca who lived at 1515 Bonnie Brae Place in River Forest. Ricca was, without a doubt, one of the most important, if not THE most important mob figures in Chicago, overseeing all operations in the state of Illinois.

The third Crime Boss in the picture was Sam Giancana. What wasn't known at the time is that Sam Giancana and President John Fitzgerald Kennedy shared three things in common. One, they both knew that the 1960 presidential election was fixed when the mob came through with the votes in Chicago. Nixon, in spite of carrying 93 of the 102 counties in Illinois, somehow lost Illinois by a total of 8,858 votes, thus securing Illinois' 27 electoral votes and the Presidency for Kennedy, thanks to Mr. Giancana. Two, was a hatred of Fidel Castro in Cuba. The third was that they were both sleeping with the same woman, Judith Exner, who they used to transfer large sums of money from JFK to Giancana to fund the *Let's Kill Castro* program that never got done.

Now, not far from O'Hare airport in Schiller Park was Mannheim Road that offered up the Sahara Inn, Lido, Air Host, Orlando's Hideaway, Concord, Guest House, Golden Cleaver and other alluring places up and down what was called Glitter Gulch.

You may recall the Al's Grill baseball bat beating story discussed earlier where *"Arado, 47, owner of an Oak Park dry cleaning shop, told The Tribune last night that he had received the $10,500 in a cashier's check bearing the name of Ariola as a payment on Mannheim road* property that he sold to a "motel syndicate" in 1957. Arado said he expected to receive the final payment next year on the purchase price of $38,500."

That was the start of the Glitter Gulch project and it was all funded by union pensions controlled by the Outfit and run by Sam Giancana. As kids, we all remember our mom's driving out that way to buy eggs and produce from the farmers out there, long before the A&P, or Jewel T opened their grocery stores. But then came Glitter Gulch, as well as the expansion of O'Hare Airport, and the farms quickly disappeared.

Which brings up a fourth boss named Manny Skar. He owned Manny Skar's Sahara Inn on the Mannheim Strip where just about every top name Vegas entertainer performed. Even the Beatles once stayed there. Skar, for whatever reason, sold the 267 room, $10.8 million establishment to the singing cowboy, Gene Autry in 1963. Manny later decided he wanted it back, but Autry said 'No'. So, in July of 1963, a small bomb went off at the Sahara Inn doing little damage. Autry still said 'No.' But on January 17, 1964 a car bomb rocked the Sahara Inn as well as neighboring buildings and blew out a few windows. Fortunately, no one was hurt. Only this time, Autry said 'Yes' and sold it back to Manny Skar. Skar wanted more than anything to dominate the Mannheim Strip with his Sahara Inn which he pretty much pulled off, working with Rocco Pranno, who controlled Schiller Park, Franklin Park, Melrose Park, Stone Park, and Northlake. Plus, Mr. Pranno was the President of Manny Skar's Sahara Motel Corporation. The Sahara Inn was truly Las Vegas comes to Chicago. The Sahara Inn opened on January 6, 1962 with Bobby Darin as the headliner performing to a sellout crowd. But then, three years later on September 11, 1965, the Chicago Tribune ran this story:

"Manny Skar, 42, was gunned down in gang-fashion shortly before 1am today behind the 17 story apartment building in which he lived at 3800 N. Lake Shore Drive.

A volley of gunshots rang out as he stepped from the garage and he was hit in the right eye, left cheek, chest and right knee. His body was taken to the morgue.

Last December, federal agents arrested Skar for evading $417,472 in taxes on $1,381,320 he allegedly earned between 1960 and 1963. A hearing was pending.

Last spring, Skar was subpoenaed by a federal grand jury investigating organized crime in Chicago."

Long story short, Skar was "whacked" in a mob hit shortly before he was to turn over evidence regarding the "Chicago Outfit" to federal authorities. The "whacking" was attributed to mobster Joey "The Clown" Lombardo. You may remember him also from the

Al's Grill baseball bat beating incident a few pages back. (Yes, it really is difficult to keep track of all these guys!)

So, in case there is any doubt about the connection between the mob, Glitter Gulch and Vegas, it disappeared when every top named Vegas entertainer performed up and down the Mannheim strip including Frank Sinatra, Dean Martin, Count Basie, Nelson Riddle, Martha Raye, Phyliss Diller, Louis Prima and Keely Smith, Zsa Zsa Gabor, Bobby Darin, Georgie Jessel, Ella Fitzgerald, Dinah Shore, Sammy Davis, Jr., Patti Page, Jackie Mason, Jack Carter, Vic Damone, and Fred Waring to name but a few.

Only now it's July of 1973. CBS had sold the Yankees to George Steinbrenner back in January. The undefeated Miami Dolphins remained undefeated beating the Redskins in the Super Bowl; Nixon and Agnew were sworn in for a second term, then Agnew went, Watergate broke and quickly became the number one topic of discussion; the World Trade Center officially opened in New York City, but Chicago's own Sear's Tower had the bragging rights of being the World's Tallest Building; some delivery company called Federal Express opened for business; George Foreman put a world of hurt on Joe Frazier to take the heavyweight title; Secretariat became the first triple crown winner since 1948 by winning the Belmont by 31 lengths; and the first televised war that we'd been watching nightly for the past ten years, Viet Nam, finally came to an end and friends, relatives, and POWs began coming home. A great many of our friends and relatives had already come home, either in body bags or mentally not quite right.

Also, by 1973 much had changed for the mob. In 1968, Title III of the Omnibus Crime Control and Streets Act was introduced, zeroing in on organized crime. And that was followed by the Organized Crime Control Act of 1970. So, by 1973, the mob in Chicago was merely a shadow of its former self and near extinction. Sam Giancana had moved to Mexico, while the Big Boss, Paul Ricca died in 1972, before Giancana made his return back to Chicago in 1975. But then, I'm getting ahead of myself. Joe Accardo, who had replaced his brother Tony, was pretty much retired. Marshall Caifano, a top executioner for the Outfit had been running the Outfit since Giancana left for Mexico. During the mob's decline, they were losing interest in some of the less lucrative suburbs, like River Grove, while others like Elmwood Park, Maywood, Melrose Park, Rosemont, Stone Park, etc remained on their radar.

Several of the Western Suburbs were, for the most part, controlled by what was left of the mob from River Forest with lesser bosses controlling individual suburbs. But both River Grove and Elmwood Park were ruled over by Mr. DiFronzo who actually lived in River Grove. Elmwood Park's Village President, alias Mayor Elmer Conti controlled both River Grove and Elmwood Park on behalf of Mr. DiFronzo, only the powers that be in River

Forest no longer had much interest in River Grove. Chief of Police O'Hallen, the former mob enforcer for both towns was retired. Attorney Harry Steigerwaldt, Sr. was the mouthpiece for the mob in River Grove. The problem was that Harry Steigerwaldt, Sr. had a touch of Manny Skar sized ego in him and had delusions of grandeur. He wanted to take River Grove back on behalf of the Outfit whether the Outfit wanted it back or not figuring there was no one to really stop him. There was little doubt that chaos was on its way that would drive many to join the "Battle for River Grove." And Harry's first assault was only weeks away.

As for White's Tavern, not much changed. It still reeked of failure and smelled of decaying lives. Every patron was a story in and of him or herself, and every one of them living on what appeared to be an empty dream of hope.

Sweat. Thick, foul smelling sweat just rolled off arms like lubricating oil. Sweat soaked shirts and blouses clung to bodies like a wet suit. The clientele was sprawled out everywhere. Inside, outside, on top of cars, sitting on the front stoop, passed out in booths, or doing strange, usually criminal things in the bathrooms.

The pungent, often mephitic odor of heavy perspiration, cheap perfume, stale beer, and urine permeated the air. Thick smoke strangled lungs and burned eyes as *Scotch & Soda*, *My Kind of Town*, *Gonna Turn My Brown Eyes Blue*, *LeRoy Brown*, *My Way*, *Right Place Wrong Time*, or *Your Momma Don't Dance* blared from the tinny speakers of the juke box near the front door.

Even the bathrooms had character as well as characters in them. The Ladies john was always cleaner and better maintained than the Guys, so most everyone used the Ladies. You really didn't want to go into the Guys' john unless you were desperate. Oh, and Earl, in what he thought was a moment of brilliance, had installed black lights in both johns in hopes of curtailing any illegal happenings taking place in them. Wrong Answer!! Thank you for playing! Turned out that the black lights just enhanced the cocaine use that was already going on.

Dope, the number one commodity in the Tavern, sustained a livelihood for many of the Tavern patrons. Cocaine, heroin, angel dust, pot, hash, THC, LSD, hash oil, mushrooms, MDA, quaaludes, seconal, valium, amyl nitrate, uppers, downers, reds, yellows, a pill of every color were plentiful and available.

"You fuckin Jagoff!"

"Can I help it if I gotta sneeze!?!"

"If I bust your fuckin nose, ya think it might help!?!"

"C'mon asshole!"

Hey!! Hey!!! Would you two sweethearts knock it off down there!?! I don't want any fights in here tonight, I got enough of that goin' on upstairs! "

"Look Earl, this piece of shit just sneezed a dime hit of coke off the fuckin table!"

"You schmucks are gonna land me in jail, yet! Just let it go, Bill!"

It really wasn't the money as much as it was the principal at stake plus his image. There was no tarnishing the image. Bill Ott was the self-appointed King of White's Tavern and Guardian of the White Powder. He was also a giant contradiction. While charming, witty, out-going, highly intelligent, and even compassionate, he was also quite persuasive, forceful, imposing, menacing, disturbing, unbalanced, unstable, deranged, and unhinged. No doubt, someone to be feared. Yet, the person who feared Bill Ott the most was Bill Ott. He hated being alone with himself. It scared him. He also craved attention. Introspection and a search of self was far too foreboding for him to attempt. Instead, he lives the lies he creates and believes every one of them. The original meaning of the word brazen comes to mind, which was to pass your brass off as gold. It's what Bill did, passing himself off as something he really wasn't, or then again, maybe he was, but he never knew for certain. What it really came down to is that Bill Ott knew neither himself nor those around him, nor did he care. He was living life Large and always on the edge. And, he was right where he wanted to be... the center of attention.

A bar stool suddenly went airborne and slammed full force into the Ladies bathroom door. Earl, with head in hand, yelled "Now WHAT!?!" He was actually relieved it wasn't aimed at him.

"Genie, get outta that fuckin bathroom or I'm gonna beat your fuckin head in!" Donny Williams was a large man at six feet two and 222 pounds. Most of that was muscle. His girlfriend, Genie, was a petit, feisty brunette who stood all of five feet one weighing in at 103 pounds. Both wore mostly black.

"Don't even THINK of threatening me you fucking limp dick jagoff!! An enraged Genie Bocek stormed out of the bathroom and charged right toward Donnie. It was one swift motion of leaving the bathroom, advancing toward Donnie and planting her knee squarely into his groin. Donny doubled up and went down like he'd just been hit by George Foreman.

Earl just shook his head, commenting aloud to no one in particular, "Who said women were the weaker sex?"

Bill walked over to the fallen Donny Williams. "Here ya go, buddy. Have an Old Style on me. By the way, she bolted right after she kicked ya in the balls."

"Fuck her. Who gives a shit? She'll come back crying, beggin for me to take her back, I'll beat her up a little and it'll all be like old times," Donny said with a bit of a sheepish grin. "Plus, she really can suck the chrome off a trailer hitch."

The big rotating Schlitz clock with the handsome Irish woman's face that hung over the bar registered 9:32pm. The majority of the regulars wouldn't show up for another hour or two.

"Well, shit Draska, where the hell you been?"

"I been in Milwaukee."

"I been in Milwaukee and I ain't never seen you there…. Where in the hell are you going? I'm talking to you."

"I'm going to the Tavern."

"You're in the fucking tavern, you asshole."

Earl, overhearing the conversation, just shook his head and served another customer.

The police were seldom if ever called to handle any of the Tavern's problems. The only exceptions to this rule were fire, armed robbery, stabbings, beer bottle contests to see who can hit a passing motorist, major brawls occurring either inside or outside the Tavern, and those times a patron took it upon him or herself to direct traffic on Grand Avenue in front of the Tavern.

As for fights, dope, intoxication and gambling were concerned, the police had a hands-off policy when it came to the Tavern.

"Hey, Earl! How's life?"

"You need to ask somebody who has one."

Night after night, Earl Carmony mustered up the strength to hold off the invading hordes. Night after night he'd count what was in the register after closing, climb the stairs leading to the apartment above and try to convince himself it was all really worth it. After all, he owned the building and the Tavern, and was making good coin in an all-cash business... and he'd done it with a high school education.

"Christ, I was a fuckin tool and die maker working for International Harvester and now I'm a fuckin entrepreneur!" he thought to himself, which was the same thought he thought every night before heading up the stairs. Tired, shoulders drooping and with aching legs from standing so long, Earl timidly approached the door to his apartment, bracing himself for what he knew was to come. In his left hand was the box full of money. In his right was now the doorknob which he turned and opened.

"For Crissakes, Earl, sell that fuckin place and let's get outta this stinkin' shit ass town. We can go someplace nice where it's warm in winter and cool in the summer. Maybe San Diego! But, NO! You gotta spend all your fucking time in that cesspool you call a Tavern down below, ooglin' those young honeys and wishin'!"

Marge, Earl's wife of 24 years, looked tired, fed up and a bit haggard. She was a blond woman a year or two past forty. They met at a party a couple years after Earl got out of the Army and just before he started working at International Harvester. He had her by two years. Marge's face was angular, and it was easy to see she was once quite attractive, only now her prettiness was about six years past its best moment. She lifted her shoulders and hands and let them fall in a gesture of defeat.

Earl remained silent, just standing there, looking defeated himself.

"Earl, look. I'm not happy and you're not either."

"Marge, c'mon. We agreed when we started this, just another couple years. That's all. Then we'll get out of here."

She'd heard it all before, including the couple of years that was at least a couple of years ago.

"C'mon and join me downstairs. I could use the help, really."

"Earl, like I said, I'm not happy. I hate that place downstairs and I hate this place up here. I have no life. WE have no life. And, YOU have no life outside of that fucking Tavern."

As usual, nothing was resolved, and Earl headed off to bed. As he passed by his wife, he handed her the box of money. "Here, do what you want with it." And proceeded into the bathroom.

Thinking to himself, "I either fight 'em down there or battle the bitch up here. Can't win for trying."

> "I don't care about tomorrow cuz it don't matter anymore.
> People think I'm crazy or maybe just a bore.
> Now I'm not the one to argue and I'm sure they may be right
> Cuz I'm stoned most every morning and wasted every night.
> But for those of you complaining kindly leave my head alone
> For I'm the one I'm hurtin' and in this Tavern I am home." *Author Anon*

• CHAPTER THREE •

Bill was seated at the bar talking to his girlfriend, Elaine, who was about 5'7", more handsome than beautiful with a slender, very shapely, athletic body, short blond hair, a beautiful complexion, long legs, and a set of playful blue eyes that were alive with excitement. Her voice was deep and powerful for a woman, much like Jane Fonda's or Lauren Bacall's before her. And like Bill, she could light up a room with her smile. Also, like Bill, she was funny, fearless, highly intelligent and had a lightning quick, sharp, cutting wit. The most notable thing they had in common is that they both loved living on the edge. Put either Elaine or Bill in the company of The Tavern and boy did they shine, especially together. When it came to feelings though, Elaine wore her heart on her sleeve.

"Elaine, you wanna grab something to eat later?"

"Well, the short answer is No, Bill. The long answer is Hell No. By the way, I think Mr. Apt is trying to get your attention."

Bill glanced over at the Flash 90 bowling machine. It was an interesting and fun game where you slid a metal puck across a sawdust powdered lane, like a miniature bowling lane, that had wires protruding that could sense where the puck was in relationship to the pins. The object, just like in bowling, was to throw a strike for which you were given 90 points on the scoreboard. Standing next to the machine, holding a quarter up and staring at Bill was the meticulously dressed Ray Apt, with his 20-inch arms bulging out through his Banlon knit shirt wearing a shit faced grin, beckoning Bill to play a game.

His full name was Raymond J. Apt. His friends called him Ray, his foes called him Mr. Apt. Ray had an uncanny ability of spotting the best and weakest points in his victims. He was an inch, perhaps two over six feet, powerfully built, and always walked with a purpose, advancing straight at you with a slight stoop of the shoulders like a boxer, head forward and a fixed from-under stare which made you think of a charging bull. He weighed in around 230 pounds, had a 30-inch waist, short-cropped hair and a handsome face. His voice was deep, but very soft spoken, and his manner displayed a kind of dogged self-assertion which had nothing aggressive in it until there was. He was spotlessly neat, immaculate and meticulous. All told, he was built like a forklift and every bit as powerful. Ray's primary occupation was to hurt people while collecting debts, making things right that were wrong, and convincing people of things about which they really didn't want to be convinced. When it came time for that, the "tell" was that his eyes became slits, narrow and a bit sultry. Ray's favorite expression was telling someone *"We're about to have a man to victim talk."*

"Hey, Otto! You want in?"

Actually, Ray Apt was one of the more complex characters in the Tavern. In addition to his physical attributes, he was highly intelligent and a bit of a Theologian. Just as Earl was an anachronism, Apt was a combination paradox and sociopath. He'd spend hours studying people and life. He had an insatiable hunger to learn more about the thoughts and wisdom of such greats as Kant, Hegel, Schopenhauer, Kierkegaard, Wittgenstein, Husserl, Heidegger, Sartre and especially Nietzsche, as Ray himself was pretty much a fatalistic existentialist. Ray delighted in conversing at great length about the philosophies of these men; his own personal philosophy; or the art of hitting a person, causing as much damage as possible per blow. There was no doubt that Ray was every bit as deadly as a rusty nail.

"Hey, Otto! I'm talking to you. You in or not?!?"

"You fuckin loser! Hell yes, I'm in!! I'll beat your fuckin ass again, which reminds me, where's the $200 you owe me, ya motherfucker?"

"You mean $300.00"

Bill, giving Ray a look of curiosity and doubt says, "Raymond. In the sacred words of the Virgin Mary, come again?"

"I need to borrow another hundred. But I got a quarter for this fuckin game."

Bill, glancing back at Elaine, "C'mon over E and watch me destroy this broke fuck."

"Hi, Ray. How's your business going?"

"What business?"

"Dial a beating."

"Cute, Elaine. Very cute."

Ray inserted the quarter, pushed the player button and the machine came to life indicating 'Two'. "Flash or Strike Ninety?" "Flash, and I'll go first. It's your quarter but my two-hundred."

"Three-hundred."

Bill pushed the heavy metal puck back and forth to establish his rhythm as the red circular electric light passed back and forth across the lane and in front of the pins. On the eighth repetition, Bill released the puck.

"Flash, motherfucker! That's six hundred points already!"

"Fuck you! It's a ten-frame game and I ain't shot yet."

Bill, while waiting for Ray to take his shot sipped a rum and coke that looked more like a CC and Seven.

"Earl, would you turn up the fuckin air conditioner for Crissakes? I'm dying in here."

"Die Otto, die." With that Earl wrung a pool of sweat onto the floor from his sweat soaked t-shirt.

"Earl, you only need one thing to prove you're an asshole."

"And, what's that, Bill?"

"A chance."

"Go fuck yourself."

"Drunk last night, drunk the night before, tonight I'm gonna get drunk like I never got drunk before."

• CHAPTER FOUR •

"So, what do you think?"

"You call yourself a writer? You can't dot the "I" in the word shit! Plus, you left out a lot."

"Then fill in the gaps and talk about it in your interview," as I place two Sony digital recorders that are slightly larger than a deck of cards on the table, hit the record button and say, "Most of what you're about to hear actually happened."

"What the fuck! I'm not doing any fucking interview. You already know all about me, you know all the players, you know all the stories. Christ, you've known me since first fuckin grade. What!?! "

Interviewer looks at him with a quizzical, doubtful, disappointed look.

"Ok. Hello. My name's Bill Ott and I am truly the Bad Example. I fucked up. I had a full ride wrestling scholarship to Ball State and sometime during my sophomore year walked off campus and never went back. If there was a right way to do things, I found it too damn hard, so I always went in the opposite direction. And, if I had a choice between two evils, I always picked the one I hadn't tried yet. I ruined my relationship with my kid. I ruined my marriage. I've pissed off most of my friends. I've been a huge disappointment to most everyone and now I'm here. Which is a surprise in itself since the over and under on my life expectancy was only forty. Ok? Interview over?"

Fighting his thoughts and emotions, Bill tapped his foot slightly, bit his lip for a moment, set fire to a cigarette, and pocketed the lighter. A lightning shaped vein began pulsing along his temple before he flung his words out at me.

"Ok, asshole" Bill says while staring at the two recorders, "Ya know when you're young and you got the world by the balls cuz everything seems to be going your way, not to mention that you think you're smarter than everyone else? Not saying anyone is stupid, or nothing. Well, that was me in 1973, the King of White's Tavern. I had it all. I literally made millions and blew every dime of it. I had women. I had Elaine. I had Devin. And I pissed it all away cuz I never thought about tomorrow. You know, why worry about tomorrow when today is so far off? Truth be told I really didn't care. I could give a fuck about the money, the women, or even Elaine and Devin. I only cared about the ride. It was always all about the rush, the excitement and living on the edge and fuck the cost. But ya know what? I can't imagine doing anything else. Hell, I don't even know how to do anything else, and I wouldn't want to, either. I did what I did because I was good at it and my life is a disaster because of it. All told, I was Chairman of the Board of Irresponsible People. Pretty much, end of story."

"Let's go back to when you walked off campus at Ball State."

"What of it? "

"It reminded me of the night before your final meet in high school. You were ranked number one in the state at 165 pounds and the night before your match, I saw you in the hotel with a cigarette in one hand and a beer in the other at ten o'clock at night. And the next day you lost the match."

"Hey. It's what I do. What you just said defines me. It defines my life, which is what I'm trying to tell you."

"Let me ask you. How will you know when you've died?"

"Easy. When it all stops being fun."

"Has it?"

"Ok, jagoff. As you know I got right with Jesus and into reading the Bible much later in life and gotta say that story of Jonah inside the fuckin whale really hit me. That motherfucker ended up inside that whale because he was running away from his responsibilities. That one hit home because I never saw myself *having* any responsibilities. Elaine used to leave Devin with me to babysit. What a fuckin mistake that was. Devin was like two and pretty much, so was I."

"You attribute that to your drug dealings, or what?"

"Look" says Bill, "If you weren't there, you gotta understand that in the early 70s, drugs were the hottest thing going and reality was for those who couldn't face their fantasies. In terms of drug related crime, it was wild. Absolutely fuckin wild! And back then, if you were looking for marijuana, you were probably looking for me and Brian King. We had really fresh Columbian and could sell it at a price that was pretty irresistible."

Historically speaking, Bill's drug business actually began in 1942 when Douglas Aircraft built Orchard Field Airport to manufacture C-54 planes during WWII. Which is why, if you fly in or out of O'Hare, your ticket reads ORD. In 1949, Orchard Field was renamed in honor of Congressional Medal of Honor winner and Navy Pilot, Edward O'Hare who appropriately for Chicago, was the son of "Artful" Eddie O'Hare who managed the Outfits Wall Street investments. Only, "Artful" Eddie opened his mouth to the Feds and some shotgun blasts closed it for him. It wasn't long before the City of Chicago outgrew Midway Airport located in Cicero and opened a commercial facility at O'Hare. Then in 1963, President Kennedy appropriately attended the dedication ceremony for the new terminal, since it was Chicago and the mob that put him in office. Truth be known, O'Hare Airport and Chicago's crossroads location had a lot to do with Bill's highly profitable business ventures. The key was to tie in with the airlines, especially Eastern working baggage, know which package, suitcase or duffel bag contained the goods, and switch them with an identical looking empty.

"It wasn't long before we went from selling lids to one-pound bricks, which is how I got caught in my motor home by the fuckin Cook County Sheriffs with three-hundred one-pound bricks of weed inside. Fuckin jagoffs. Ya gotta wonder how long that haul stayed in the evidence locker."

"You got off though with a pretty light sentence."

"Are you fuckin' kidding?? The lawyer took ten large and the fucking judge took another fifteen-grand and I still had three months in Joliet plus, two-years probation. You call that fuckin' light?"

Bill passes his hand over his forehead and hair, at least what little is left of it before proceeding. I could see some sweat beading up along his brow and upper lip.

"Fuck, it's hot in here!" He takes a swig of water before continuing.

"Yeh, it was, after all Chicago. Lawyers, judges, and cops were on the take. Hell, if you had to, you could buy off a witness and tamper with a jury. If you had enough money, you could pretty much get away with anything, and I mean anything. Look money isn't everything in Chicago, but then again neither is anything else."

"You remember that Greybeard Sting Operation in eighty-three when they caught all those judges in Chicago on the take?"

"My point, exactly." He takes another sip of water.

"Anyway, the whole time we're doing the marijuana, the same guy who put me on to that now asks me if any of my friends might like some cocaine. I give him a big smile and say, yeh, ME! Next thing I know, he hands me an ounce of the stuff, tells me I can cut it with powder to increase my profits and then shows me how to do it. Then of course, we snorted it. It ain't long before I'm buying a scale and my first kilo of coke. Back then, you could get a kilo for about fifty-thousand, which was still a ton of money. But, you stood to make fifteen-to-twenty thousand on top of that fifty. The biggest fuckin problem Brian and I had is that between the two of us, we were shoving about ten thousand of that fifteen-to-twenty thousand up our own noses! You ever hear that old expression, I can resist anything but temptation? Well, that was me and Brian.

Bill laughs with that big, charming grin still in place.

"Later on, I hooked up with a guy making these absolutely gorgeous redwood coffee tables out in California. These things were fuckin beautiful. And they weren't cheap, either. He'd ship 'em outta California to all over the United States. And we'd pack anywhere from 1 to 10 kilos of coke into each and every one of those motherfuckers. We never did get caught. Yeh, the Seventies were great and if you were buying coke, marijuana or hash back then, you were probably buying it through me and Brian. Only, it wasn't as rough, big or as bad as that business is today. It's a whole nuther world out there today."

"Is that why you got stabbed in the arm?"

Bill gets a sheepish grin and shows me the hole or deep indentation in his arm just below the very faded tattooed mouse he had done his senior year in high school. "Yeh, and that was in Miami the year before our honeymoon. They were trying to stab me in my chest but I got the better of the three of them, fucking assholes. I think they were college kids."

"How'd they know you were dealing?"

"I was in a bar, by myself, which was stupid, playing pool with these guys. I must've said something I shouldn't have."

"They get the drugs?"

"I didn't have any, I had money."

"They get the money?"

"Some."

Bill looks at me with a sly expression. "You know what a pyrrhic victory is?"

"Yeh. When the win wasn't worth it."

"Well, it wasn't worth it to those three. Whatever money they got from me either went to pay for a dental bill or setting a broken arm, the fucks."

Bill was getting heated just thinking about it.

"Hey! Can I get something to drink?"

He's handed another bottle of water.

"That's fuckin it!?! Jesus!"

Bill downs the bottle in one gulp.

"You know, me and Brian did pretty well over the years. Blew it all, but still did pretty well. So, how about Brian? You ever interview him?"

"Yeh, and he's a lot bigger now."

"How does a guy six feet eight, four-hundred-pounds get any bigger than that?"

"Easy. He now weighs five-hundred and fifty-pounds."

"Jesus!"

"I interviewed him at White's."

• CHAPTER FIVE •

Brian King was about the size of Mt. Rushmore. Fortunately, Brian was pretty jovial until he wasn't. Like when someone shorter than he decides they just have to take him on. Brian had two favorite expressions. The first was, "The Bigger they are, the harder they maul." The second was, "The Bigger they are, the bigger the beating you're gonna get."

Back in 1973, Brian was still a svelte three-hundred pounds, donning a long pony tail, a full beard, an American flag headband, steel toed boots, bib overalls and a tuxedo shirt he stole from his brother's wedding. He wasn't one to be missed inside White's Tavern.

"Fuckin mosquitoes!"

"What the fuck, man. You gonna pitch or swat?"

White's was getting quite crowded and *H. O. T.*, Hot! As both sweat and tempers flared, more and more of the clientele took to the outdoors, seeking relief from the heat and humidity inside. Outside wasn't much better.

"How about we pitch quarters for a buck a shot at ten feet and liners pay double?"

"Fuckin-A, Brian. It's ten feet for us and more like five feet to you! Make it fifteen feet."

It was a small group of five contestants with another dozen or so spectators.

"Fifteen it is!" Glancing over at Skip Moline who was standing by his fourteen-year-old Ford Falcon. "Hey Skip, turn your headlights on and shed some light on this game of chance we're about to play."

Other than Brian, Bill, and Raymond, few if anyone was making more than fifteen grand a year. It didn't matter to anyone in White's how much money you made or what you did for a living. But spending money was what you did at White's.

Holding up a twenty and towering over everyone Brian announced, "And gentlemen, just to let you know what kind of stand-up guy I am, I'm buying the first round of Old Styles if someone's willing to go back in there and get 'em. Oh, and I shoot last!"

"Fuck, you, I'll go." said Denny Posen, as he grabbed the twenty out of Brian's paw. "Old Style, by all means!" Not only was Posen a beer truck driver for Old Style, but his other claim to fame was his passing the test and being accepted to the Chicago Police Academy. The problem was that he never joined. "It was too much fuckin pressure."

"Ok, so while you're getting the beers, I'm gonna shoot." The words belonged to Davey Joe McLaughlin, Ray Apt's part-time accomplice in clearing out neighborhood bars. On nights, much like this one, Ray and Davey Joe would enter a strange bar and just take on everyone and anyone willing to fight them. Well, actually they took on everyone whether they were willing to fight them or not.

Davey's philosophy was always, "Hey, if you hit your friends, they won't stay your friends. If I hit my boss, I'm gonna get fired. So, I hit strangers."

All told, Davey was a big, good looking, fighting, fucking, and drinking machine.

"I'm up after you, Davey." Fat Joe was a fireplug with feet. He was about as tall as he was wide and had two careers. He earned about $8,500.00 as a factory worker and another $10,000.00 forging and cashing checks he'd stolen out of people's mailboxes. Only Fat Joe usually just gave the check forging money away.

"Gee, Joe, all the girls are going down to Florida for a week and I ain't got the bread to go with them."

"No problem, Cheryl." The next day, Cheryl Johnson had anywhere from $300-$500 in cash from Joe that she was never expected to repay in either cash or favors. Or, if a group decided to hit Slicker Sam's in Melrose Park for dinner, you could count on Joe picking up the tab.

"Then I'm going after Fat Joe." said Jim Macatelli, alias Yukon Jack. Mac could consume enough booze in one night to kill half the residents in Evanston. Mac was built like Baretta, and started dressing like him, too. When he bought the fuckin' parrot to go with the clothes though, everyone knew he'd lost it.

"What in the fuck are you gonna do with a goddamn parrot?"

"He's gonna sit on my shoulder, just like Baretta."

"He's gonna shit on your shoulder just like Baretta, only they don't show that on television."

"I'll wear a towel."

"Towel or no towel, that fuckin parrot ain't comin in here!" That was Earl's edict.

Davey Joe's quarter glimmered in the headlights of Skip Moline's car as it flew from his thumb and index finger hitting the pavement on its side. "Shit! The damn thing's gonna roll!!"

"Man, look at the loop that things making."

"Holy Crap, would ya look at that!?! A goddamn liner."

"Fuck you, Davey Joe!"

"No. Fuck you, Macatelli. Liners pay double and I dare ya to beat it!"

"Come get 'em while they're cold, ladies. Compliments of Brian." Denny Posen was back with the beers.

"Are you peckin' my ass? Davey tossed a liner?!?"

Running down Grand Avenue approaching White's Tavern from the West was Sam Kunkel.

"HEY!!" As the saying goes, 'Great Messages Make the Messenger Great' and Sam Kunkel was not going to lose out in getting his place in the parade of history's great messengers.

"HEY!!"

"Who the fuck's yelling?"

Skip Moline was squinting to see if he could make out who the mysterious messenger was.

"Sounds like Kunkel."

"Well, tell him to shut the fuck up. I'm trying to concentrate on my toss here and he's distracting me."

Out of breath and perspiring a little more than the others, Sam Kunkel finally made it across Grand Avenue arriving at his final destination, White's Tavern.

"Didn't ya hear me yelling?!?"

"Everyone in Elmwood Cemetery could hear you yelling, and they're all dead!"

"I'm telling ya, Ronnie Williams has gone nuts!"

"Oh, call the fuckin Daily News already! RW not only IS nuts, but he's always been nuts."

"I'm telling you he's on top of Al's Grill throwing beer bottles at cars!"

"Shit! Two inches off the line."

"Nice shot, Joe, but not close enough."

"Ah, fuck you guys! Is Donny and Bobby in there?" looking towards White's.

"I'm sure they are."

With that bit of information, Sam pulled the well beaten back door screen door open and entered blurting out his big announcement.

"HEY!", he screamed over the deluge of noise permeating the tavern.

"HEY!! Ronnie Williams' is on top of Al's Grill throwing beer bottles at cars and Tarpey's comin to arrest him!!"

"They ain't full, are they?"

"Nah. I'm sure he drank 'em first."

Al's Grill was a greasy, small, four stool hamburger joint with a flat roof, right down the block from the Tavern. It was also kind of an historical landmark in River Grove thanks to the pinball machine, mob and baseball bat incident years ago. So, at least, Ronnie chose a historical site to put on a show.

"Well, that fuckin jagoff, Ronnie. He had to go and end our game just when I had a fuckin liner."

"Yeh, tough luck, Davey."

"Fuckin, A! Would ya look at Ronnie in his fuckin skivvies!!"

"The sunglasses and boots add a nice touch, though."

"You goddamnmutherfuckercocksuckingsonofabitchinasshole, take this!!"

"Holy Shit, that beer bottle just exploded when it hit the pavement!

"Oh, shit! Here's Tarpey."

Tom Tarpey had just been named police chief of River Grove. He had joined the force in his late twenties and knew most of the White's Tavern clientele since they were young, juvenile delinquents.

Speaking through a bullhorn, Tarpey called out, "Ok, Ronnie, put down the beer bottles and c'mon down from there."

"Chief!! Great to see ya!!

"Ronnie, stay away from the edge. I don't want you falling off of there."

It was obvious to all that Ronnie's balance was not the best and that he was staggering more than just a little.

"C'mon up, Tom and have a beer with me!"

Funny how someone can make a complicated situation so simple. Tarpey merely walked around the back, ascended the ladder and met a very plastered RW at the top.

"Hey, Chief! Let me help you up!" as Ron extended his outstretched hand.
The crowd below was losing interest and began heading back to White's.

"So, Ronnie. Ya know I gotta take you in, but what in the hell did you think you were doing up here?"

"Look, Chief. Between the job, the weather and the old lady, I'd had it. I just hadda get all fucked up and let off some steam. Butchya know what?"

"What?"

"I'm glad it's over. I was runnin outta beer and energy. Now I'm just tired, drunk and bored. Can I go home?"

"Sure, Ron, after a night in jail where you can sober up. C'mon, let's go."

"And, ya know what else?"

"What's that Ronnie?"

"I have a great respect for the law."

"Well, Ronnie," Tarpey chuckled, "that at least makes two of us in River Grove that does. Now let's go."

Tarpey assisted the partially clad Ron Williams down the fire escape to the cheers and boos of the few onlookers remaining below. After placing Ron in the backseat of his squad car, Tarpey went back up to the roof to retrieve Ronnie's clothes and whatever beer was left.

"Oh, well. Another criminal apprehended!"

"Look, Tom. A lot of us taxpayers think you give these out-of-control kids way too much slack and something needs to be done about it."

"Mr. Warchol, what brings you down over here to this end of town?"

"All the commotion. Plus, I was on my way home when a beer bottle exploded just missing my car. You know Tom that it's our taxes that pay your salary."

"Well, Mr. Warchol, if anything should happen to you, including being hit by a flying beer bottle while I'm Chief of Police, you have my word that I'll see to it that you get a full refund. Now, have a good night, be careful going home and I've got work to do here."

"Ok, whose toss?"

"Fuck you, Davey Joe. That game's history. We're playing a new one."

"No fuckin way!"

"Way!"

"Here's five bucks. Go buy a round!"

Davy Joe was now glaring at Brian King. "Ya know, Brian? You ain't so big, you're just tall, that's all!"

"Davey Joe, I assure you, you don't want any part of what I'm about to give you. Now take the ten and go get us some Old Styles."

Davey Joe ripped the fin from Brian's paw and went back into the bar. "Earl!! Five Old Styles!! And keep the change!!"

The heat and humidity climbed steadily with no relief in sight as gallons of beer sweat encapsulated bodies in an attempt to cool the skin and tempers. *Dago T's,* the two-strap t-shirt, later referred to as Wife Beater's, were drenched in perspiration as were bowling shirts, blouses, tank tops and underwear.

"Earl!! For godsakes, do something with that fuckin air conditioner!! It's hotter than a fuck in here!"

• CHAPTER SIX •

"Ok, Brian, I'm all set. Let's get on with this interview. So, in addition to being Bill's partner which didn't land you in jail, you had a second career that did land you in Joliet for of all things, breaking and entering. It isn't often that a guy your size is a Cat Burglar."

"I wasn't a Cat Burglar. I was just really good at breaking into buildings."

"I'm the idiot here because personally, I wouldn't have a clue how to break into a building without getting caught. I'd imagine you have to know a lot about a building before you break into it. I mean, you can't just show up and do what you do without knowing ahead of time what you're in for."

"Look. The way it worked is that I'd go to a place we wanted to hit and apply for a job that I usually got. Didn't really matter what the job was because I just wanted inside. So, I'm working there and checking the place out and asking a lotta questions. I'm not only getting the lay of the land, but I'm getting a lotta of my questions answered. One of our favorite targets was any place that was close to the forest preserves. That way, we could lose ourselves in the woods, either during or after the heist. During meant we was in trouble. And we also planned most of our scores over a holiday weekend because it gave us that one extra day. "

"So, what's it take to break into a building and not get caught?"

"Look, to break into a building you need a team of guys. We had a *Bug Man*, which is an alarm guy, who could get through any alarm ever invented. We had a kid who could break into a car and drive it off faster than if ya actually had the keys to it. And we always had a couple of lookouts to watch out for cops. We also had a van. After we disarmed the alarm, we'd cut a hole in the roof, which is how we'd get into the place. We'd drop inside the building with ropes and open the doors to the loading dock. Then we'd drive the van in which had all of our equipment. You know what a burning bar is?"

"Hell, no."

"It's a long steel tube filled with alloy wire. It looks like a lance. The way it works is you heat up the end of the bar with an acetylene torch until it gets really hot. Then you open up that control valve and that blast of pure oxygen really does its job. As long as you keep injecting pure oxygen into the burning bar and keep the pressure just right, this thing gets hotter than a motherfucker and can burn through anything. Like a vault, for instance."

"Oh, shit!"

"It's actually more complicated than that, but that'll give you an idea. So, in this last caper, we bring in the burning bar and started cutting into the vault. The only problem with a burning bar is the damn thing smokes. I mean it fucking SMOKES! The flame on this thing is like 4-5 feet! Which is why I saved the most important guy for last. Our safe man could peel a safe open, chisel it or burn it with a burning bar. And you sure as hell better know what you're doing with that burning bar."

Brian gets a quizzical look on his face and asks, "You know anything about safes?"

"Like I said before, Brian. I'm the idiot here. This is all new to me. No, I sure as hell, don't."

"Not all safes are the same because they're not all made outta the same stuff. Those fuckin stainless-steel safes were always the hardest to open cuz you had to burn 'em. But you had to be careful how you burned them. They had a layer of copper in them. So, while you're burning the safe, the copper melts and reseals the area you just burned making your progress zero while pissing you off! The only fucking way to cut through one of these safes is with a burning bar. Man, to see a burning bar cut through a safe like that was like spreading cream cheese on a bagel."

"So, I'm gonna guess you used a burning bar on this last job you did."

"Oh, did we ever. Only, I don't know why, but the smoke from the burning bar got so bad this time that we hadda open every fuckin door and window in the place just so we could just friggin' breathe."

"Holy, Crap!"

"Picture this. It's 2am, smoke is pouring outta every fuckin door and window in the place like the place is on fire and here comes a patrol car. The goddamn lookout fell asleep and it was pure luck I spotted the car. So, we're running around like a bunch of crazed junkyard dogs shutting all the doors and windows, thinking we're fucked. I'm telling you, it was bedlam. We grabbed everything we could and we took off into the woods. Like I said before, I like to hit places near the Forest Preserves."

"Were you nervous?"

"Nervous!?! Fuckin AY!! I swore I was gonna have a heart attack or shit in my pants, or both."

"Then what did you do?"

Not a whole helluvalot we could do. We were watching the fuckin cop car figuring he's gotta be calling in help, but the sonofabitch just keeps driving and leaves. Never even gets outta the car to inspect a goddamn thing. How he couldn't see that smoke seeping out is still beyond me."

"Sounds like your lucky day. Were you breathing easier?"

"Oh, hell yes! So, we grab everything we dragged into the woods and go back inside the building. We finally cut the safe in half, open it and stuff all the dough in canvas sacks. The driver backs the van up close to the vault and we stuff it with these bags full of cash and take off."

"How much?"

"Turns out we scored somewhere's around $175,000.00. All cash."

"Wow! So, what's the secret to breaking into a building besides what you already told me?"

"Look, when you attack a building like this, and I mean attack, you gotta see that the fucking things alive. It's us against the building and you better give each building some respect. Plus, I gotta tell ya it's one helluvan adrenaline rush."

"What would you say is the most important thing?"

"The crew. Without a doubt, the crew. Each member of the crew is a finely tuned specialist and absolutely fuckin fanatical about his trade, with the exception of an occasional stupid lookout who falls asleep. And we all gotta work together. It's all about precision timing. The thing is, ya can't dismantle a building all at once. Ya gotta go at it a little at a time, piece by piece until you're in. And the fuckin building is talking to you the entire time saying, 'Ok Jagoff, you made it through one barrier, but I got more.' So, you get through one more and it says, 'Yeh, Asshole. You beat my security system, but you'll never get past my safe.' When we're done, and the safe has been opened and cleaned out, that building just dies right there in front of you. You feel like St. George slaying the fucking dragon or something. All that really remains of that building is the money we just took from it, only, ya know what? It's never enough. I mean it's NEVER fuckin enough because you always want more."

"More money or more adrenalin rushes?"

"Yes!"

"How'd this particular heist end?"

"We got caught. So, I did my time in Joliet and..." pausing "Did you know that me and Apt were in there at the same time and didn't even know it?"

"Yeh, he told me that. Bree was in there too. Small world, hunh?"

"Anyway, I got out 10 years later and came out a new man. Completely rehabilitated and finally ready to play it straight." Brian says with a huge laugh. "I ask you. Who in their right fuckin mind would ever believe that kinda bullshit? A day doesn't go by that I ain't looking to do another job."

• CHAPTER SEVEN •

"So, Mr. Ott, that's how Brian ended up in Joliet."

"Wow. Brian majors in breaking and entering and Ray majors in assault and battery."

"And what did you major in?"

"Fuck, you."

Bill takes a sip of water.

"You know, I was thinking of all those times we had to collect money from late payers. Neither of us ever wanted to make people pay up, but that's where Raymond came in. You know Raymond. What in the fuck I gotta tell you about him for? Go interview him and get HIS story. OMG, I can't wait to read THAT interview."

"I did that already. Actually, I interviewed him and his son, together!"

"How in the fuck could you do that?"

Ray's out. Served his time and he's out."

"No fuckin way!"

"Yeh, Way. "

"Where'd you do the interview?"

"Whites. You want to read what they had to say?"

"Fuck, yes!"

"Drinkin makes ya wander,
Wanderin makes ya gray,
So, pour me out a couple o' shots
And I'll be on my way." Paint Your Wagon.

• CHAPTER EIGHT •

"Before the conversation gets too heavy Ray, just tell me about a time you had to collect money from a guy who owed Ott money."

"You ain't getting off the hook that fuckin easy you piece a shit. Let's first talk about the time YOU paid me to collect from that guy Radtke."

Actually, it was a memory that I'd put out of my brain years ago and now felt the urge to puke. "Out of all the people you beat up and killed in your life, you still remember that one?!?! REALLY?!?"

"And it's gonna be on Tape! Turn your fuckin little recorders on, asshole."

A normal amount of traffic passed the little neighborhood bar where I told Ray that John Radtke would be. Back then, racquetball was all the rage and courts were opening up like mad. Also, back then I was what was called a copy contact, working at a downtown ad agency on Michigan Avenue. I was a damn good copywriter if I do say so myself, and Radtke had hired me as freelancer to write sales brochures and ads for a new racquetball center he had invested in. Only the sonofabitch refused to pay me, even though everything I wrote got used. First off, I was pissed. Radtke wasn't exactly a stranger to me because we once worked together at a publishing company up in Park Forest. Second off, the $350.00 he owed me was a lotta money back then. Which is why I went to Ray.

Headlights of the passing cars shed very little light on the otherwise dark parking lot situated behind the bar. Engulfed by the darkness, leaning against a new 1973 Camaro, Illinois license plate MMM487, stood the menacing Ray Apt who had a knack for stalking his victims like a cancer stalks a cell. Inside the bar, John Radtke, a thirty-five-year-old Marketing Specialist, was putting on his coat.

"Take it easy guys and I'll see ya tomorrow." "Where you going? It's still early."

"I got paperwork I gotta get done for tomorrow's meeting and I know if I stay, I'll never get to it."

"Work, work, work. That's you, John Boy!"

"Hey, if ya wanna get ahead, you gotta stick with it."

"Yeh, sure. What EVER! We'll see ya tomorrow. Be careful driving home."

"Thanks guys. Goodnight." Radtke turns and heads for the parking lot.

"Go home and do paperwork. They probably think I enjoy it", he thought to himself. "Some days I wonder. I'm fuckin 35 years old, a level twelve making twenty-nine six and the job's cost me one wife and two kids. Plus, everyone expects me to be this swinging fuckin single when I'm really a goddamn homebody. Fuckin A! Guess if it wasn't for my job, I don't know what the fuck I'd do." Radtke mumbled to himself as he headed for his car.

"Excuse me, Mr. Radtke."

"Yeh?!?" Radtke's voice cracked. Ray smelled the fear that his surprise greeting created and enjoyed it.

"Jesus H. Christ, you scared the ever lovin' shit outta me!" Trying to regain his composure, John Radtke began focusing on Ray to size him up, but between the darkness and the passing headlights, Ray appeared more like a Shape Shifter than a solid being.

"Well, since it's obvious you know who I am, who may I ask are you?"

Ray could always see well in the dark, passing headlights or not. The rods in his eyes must have outnumbered the cones, because he had great night vision. Plus, his hobby of staring down cobras at Brookfield Zoo probably contributed to his excellent eyesight. Ray was also the consummate professional. He'd been scanning Radtke's body from head to toe looking for a bulge that might divulge a weapon. No bulge. No weapon. Ray did notice Radtke's well-groomed hair, manicured nails, and good taste in expensive clothes. He figured his shoes were probably spit shined.

The silence following Radtke's question lasted less than a 'one thousand one' count but long enough for fear; a paralyzing, terrifying kind of fear to consume John Michael Radtke who knew something very bad was about to happen to him. That this was no social call.

"Lllllooook." Radtke's voice cracked. "Iiiffff ya want my wallet, my car, anything, just take it and leave me alone."

The student, Ray Apt, took great delight in knowing everything that was going on within a victim's brain and body. He knew that a massive dose of adrenaline was now coursing through Radtke's body. That the amygdala, that almond-shaped mass located deep in the brain responsible for survival related threats was now overstimulated. That Radtke's nervous system was now highly activated causing his heart rate to increase tremendously. He knew that Radtke's mouth had become dry because his body had shut down his digestive system, and that the amygdala was activating the hippocampus to tag this memory for future use. What he also knew was that this was a fight or flight moment and that Radtke would choose to run. He didn't make it. Like lightning in a bottle, Ray's first punch went to the floating rib cage cracking two. His second was a left upper cut that fractured the jaw and broke off a couple of teeth. The third punch, Ray's favorite and the one his reputation was built upon was his hard right to the nose. Cowboys used to notch their guns for the people they'd gunned down. For Ray, it was for how many noses he'd broken and Radtke had just become another notch.

Raymond J. Apt blended into the darkness and headed back to the Tavern.

It was about 27 minutes later that the unconscious John Michael Radtke was discovered lying in a small pool of his own blood next to his car. Still breathing, thank you very much, but badly in need of a hospital.

By the time he was admitted, Ray was already back at White's sipping his second rum n' coke.

"God, I hate that story!"

"Well, you hired me you fuck!"

"Yeh, but you didn't even collect the full amount."

"Hey, can I help it if the asshole only had a hundred and ten bucks in his wallet! I got my share and fees covered. Sorry you came out short." Ray chuckled as only he could.

"Ok, moving on. Tell me about a time you had to collect money from a guy for Ott."

Ray's face lights up. "Oh, shit! This one's even better than the Radtke story. Bill drives me over to this guy's house in Melrose Park who's late on a payment. So, we pull up and I get out and bang on his fuckin front door. The jagoff comes to the door, I grab him and start slapping him in the face. No sooner do I throw the guy down, then his fuckin wife jumps on me and is trying to scratch my eyes out. There's six fuckin people in the house and now they're all jumping all over me. I grab his wife and throw her through the fuckin screen door. I toss another one off the porch and busted a third guy's nose. I finally get back to the deadbeat I started with and drag his skinny ass down the porch steps to where his brand-new pickup truck is parked. I take his head and start banging it on the truck asking the motherfucker why is it he can buy a new fucking truck but can't pay his drug bill. He finally passes out and I left him lying where he fell. The rest of the group is all crying, moaning and screaming at me. I got back into Bill's car and we left. What a fuckin day that was!"

"Do you mind answering some personal questions with your son here?"

"There ain't much he doesn't already know and what he doesn't know, he should. No. Ask away."

"What's the first thing you remember about growing up?"

Before answering, Ray stares at his rum and coke for a very long second, takes a small sip, sets it down, scans the room and gives me one of his man to victim looks. There was no humor in his voice.

"Growing up my first memory was when my dad picked me up and threw me like a sixteen-inch softball. I think I kinda dipped just before I hit the wall with my face. Can you imagine that?!? Having your nose busted at age two by your own father? I remember the blood dripping. I still can't believe I didn't lose consciousness. I'll tell ya though, as soon as I could get the fuck outta that house and away from my old man, I did. I started living on the streets. I think I was maybe 11 or 12. I remember stealing clothes and blankets off people's clothes lines and I'd sleep in a cardboard box in an alley."

Ray pauses to sip his rum n' coke.

"Things got harder every day for me. I know that by the time I was twelve, I felt more like forty."

At sixteen, Ray was sent for the first time to the St. Charles Reform School and was pissed off that a fellow compatriot named John Bree had been sent there a year ahead of him. By nineteen, Ray had graduated to the Adult Correctional Institution at Joliet. The place was a notorious Illinois prison built like an old brick castle with guard towers, spirals of barbed wire and stained walls. It was a very scary place.

"When I got to Joliet the first time, all I could hear was the screaming, the talking, and the music. It all hit me, and I say's to myself, 'This is it. I'm fucked.'

"Were you?"

"Look, asshole. Joliet is not a place for the weak of heart. It's brutal."

"How about your second hitch?"

"My second time around, I was a lot older and a lot bigger. Plus, I'd done my time as a Marine in Nam so it wasn't anywhere near the same. Only this time they got me on a tougher charge. "

"Hold on, Ray. The first time at Joliet you were in for Grand Theft Auto."

"That was nuthin compared to the second time."

"So, how long was it between the first time and the second time?"

"I'm coming to that. Ya gotta understand that the first time I was just a kid. The second time I'd already been to hell and back starting with this big fuckin jungle on the other side of the fuckin planet called Nam. We were there to kill Gooks and take territory."

Ray looks at his son and continues.

"I'd read in the Stars and Stripes about how the Gooks would overtake our guys and not just kill em, but mutilate em. That really pissed me off. So, after a while, killing came easy and there was no fuckin regret about it, either. The Captain or Lieutenant or whoever the fuck was in charge would tell us to take prisoners, but ya know, we all agreed, fuck that. Ya know how many fuckin prisoners me and my guys brought back? Go ahead. Take a Scientific Wild Ass Fucking Guess."

"I'd have to say 'None."

"You're exactly fuckin right... None. Not a fuckin one. We weren't bringing back no fuckin prisoners. No way. Ya know why?"

"No, tell me."

"Cuz after a while, ya just don't care. Ya just don't give a fuck. Ya know!?!

"So, when you came back from Nam, you reunited with your brother Jimmy.

"Yeh. Ya see, we grew up in a rough area of Chicago on Leavitt Street near Holy Family Academy. It used to be all Polish, but turned pretty mixed. Mostly Puerto Rican. I think I was about 15 when I killed my first guy. Fired off a ball bearing from a sling shot. Went right through the poor bastard's temple. As kids we fucked around with zip guns, switchblades, baseball bats, you name it. And we always dabbled in petty thievery like stealing bikes, a gallon of milk, a loaf of bread, and an occasional car which is how I landed in Joliet the first time for a year."

"So, you didn't go straight to Nam after high school?"

"No, I pretty much went straight to Joliet for a year. The parole board gave me a choice a year later. Nam or another year in Joliet. I took Nam and did a tour between 1969 and 1971."

"Ok, that explains it."

"Ya know, you're a real piece a work."

"Thank you."

"Anyways, I was always real close to Jimmy, unlike my other three brothers. He and I even sorta resembled one another. Only, while I'm away in Nam, Jimmy somehow got involved with the Mob and things were getting serious for him, but I didn't know just how serious."

"First off, I never knew you had four brothers. I always thought it was just you and Jimmy."

"Oh, yeh. Two were older, then there was me, then Jimmy, then another younger one, plus we had a sister, but she died young. I think Leukemia got her. Out of the four brothers, two went straight and became auto mechanics. The one after Jimmy became an even bigger asshole than me. So, Jimmy and I got along fine."

"Only, now he's mobbed up."

"Yeh, only I didn't really know just how mobbed up he was until one night, we go out to some cheap restaurant in Melrose Park, only Jimmy suddenly disappears on me. Says he's going to the can, but then doesn't come back. I get up to look for him and find him in the fuckin parking lot."

"Something you're familiar with."

"You would know, motherfucker." Ray added with a grin.

"Anyway, I look up and here's Jimmy holding a fuckin shot gun. A shot gun for Crissakes. Only he looked about as terrified as that guy Radtke did, and his eyes looked like he was on speed. I said, 'What the fuck you doin!?!' So, I confront him and says, give me that fuckin thing and I rip it out of his hands. I was pissed. I knew he didn't know a damn thing about guns. So now I tell him to get the fuck outta here and go home. I knew why he had it, so I figured I'd wait."

"Let me get this straight. Jimmy left in the car you both arrived in and now you're in the restaurant parking lot in Melrose Park, with a shot gun, waiting for someone but you don't know who."

"Pretty much the story of my life, hunh?"

"Keep going."

"So, a car pulls up, the window goes down and the guy behind the wheel asks me, 'Where's Jimmy?' I tell him I sent him home. That he got me and don't worry about it cuz he got the best of the deal."

"Holy Crap!"

"Hey, listen to me. My brother wasn't ever made for stuff like that. Me, it was like, What the Fuck!?! You kiddin? Shoot someone? It's all I was doing for 18 months on a daily basis. I had no idea what I was supposed to do for this guy, but I really didn't give a fuck. I was just looking out for Jimmy.

Ray suddenly took a reflective pause and looked as though he was putting a great deal of thought into his next statement.

"But ya know what, it was the worst fuckin decision I ever made in my life. But, what ya gonna do. Ya gotta piss with the dick ya got."

"If you say so."

"Hey, don't get so fuckin judgmental here."

"Sorry to interrupt. Please continue."

So, I get into the backseat of the guy's car, shotgun in hand, and we drive off into the night."

"And?"

"And nuthin. End of story."

Ray never really told me what happened, but according to the Chicago Daily News, a bookie, named Al Horowitz, alias the King of Van Buren Street was no longer among the living. Al Horowitz was a handsome and very dapper dressed guy in his 50's who owned Horowitz' Restaurant on the corner of Franklin and Van Buren in the Loop. In the 40's and 50's Chicago's garment district was located in what became skid row, on West Madison. As a result, the garment district moved to West Franklin between Van Buren and Jackson. Al figured all these people had to have somewhere to eat, and he was right. You could get a corned beef sandwich on rye and place a bet on a horse without ever leaving your table. Unfortunately, Al was caught skimming even after being warned. The guy who found him came in to grab a sandwich and place a bet. He told the cops, "It was a real fuckin shock. There was Al in two fuckin pieces. His torso was on one side over there, and his legs were on the other. It's like, what the fuck!?! The guys cut in half, for God's sake. He sure as hell wasn't shot once. I stood there for a while and I looked at the mess. I took it all in, told the cops what I saw and went home knowing I had to find a new bookie."

According to the cops, THAT was the mission Ray signed up for when he decided to take the shotgun from his brother Jimmy.

"So, what happened next?"

"I get arrested. Only they sent me to Joliet while I was awaiting trial, which meant I'd be there for several months. Turns out it's the same place Brian King and Johnny Bree are in and we're there the same time only none of us knew it back then."

"So, this is now 1972?"

"Yeh."

"So what was Joliet like this time versus the last time you were in there?:

"For me, the difference between this time and the last time was that I wasn't nineteen, I was now in maximum security, which I wasn't in the last time, and killing someone was no big deal to me."

Only Joliet proved to be a key stop for Ray, taking him from troubled teen to mob enforcer.

"Look, in jail, if someone, anyone fucks with you, you gotta make an example of 'em so nobody ever wants to fuck with you again. One of the first days I'm in there, I'm in the gym. I'm already in good shape and feeling good. So, I go over to this black guy about 6'4" and he's pumping 250 pounds like it's an air mattress. So, I ask him if I can use the 25s. He says, 'Yeh Motherfucker, when I'm done'. I say's to him, You're not even using them. Let me do a set and I'll put em back. Only he ain't buyin it. He gives me a look and says, 'Hey, Motherfucker, I told you when I'm DONE.' I said, Ok. Reached down, grabbed a 25 pound plate and bopped the fuck over the head with it. The barbell he was benching is now on his throat plus he's bleeding a lot. So, I lean down and ask him if I can borrow em now, you piece a shit?"

Ray's expression goes from a smile to suddenly serious.

"Look. If you're gonna be bad, you better be very, very fucking bad and goddamn good at it. Cuz when you are, people will stay away from you on your reputation alone. There ain't no being kinda bad. You're either good at being bad or you ain't. There ain't no in between because in between will either get you badly hurt or fucking dead."

Ray takes a sip of his rum n' coke and stares directly at his son.

"Let me tell you, when ya get to Joliet ya learn quick how things work. Maximum Security was split in two. There was North State and South State. South was for the regular prisoners. North was for the wise guys who ran the prison. I mean these guys did whatever the fuck they wanted, and the warden did whatever they told him. Face it, the bastard knew he had no choice because his family would be toast if he didn't. They knew where he lived and they certainly knew where his wife and kids lived, too and that's just the way things were. So, here I am awaiting trial, and the first day I'm in there, I'm in the North State and this guy comes up to me and asks me if I want a drink. I say sure. He grabs a glass, tosses some ice in it and pours a heavy dose of scotch. You gotta understand, there ain't NO GLASSES in Prison. One of those water cooler paper things maybe, or a Dixie Cup at best, but no fuckin G L A S S, glass, especially with ice and scotch in it. So, just when I think I've seen it all, he asks me if I wanna make a phone call. WTF!?! He had his own private telephone in his fuckin cell in a Maximum Security Prison!!! These guys snuck girls in and even snuck one of the Big Wiseguy's kid in a couple times while I was there. I think it was Jackie Cerone. One guy even had a fuckin pet dog with him!! "

Ray once again goes from smile to suddenly serious.

"The one thing that became obvious to me fast is that Joliet was more of a recruiting office for the mob than anything else. They could spot talent and recruit it just like General Electric or GM. It was pretty fuckin amazing to watch."

"How'd it feel to be accepted by these guys?"

"Truthfully, it was the worst possible thing that could ever happen to me. Not only am I already a wild, insane, murderous sociopath who not only is good at it, and enjoys it, but now I'm a sociopath with power! And that suddenly makes me capable of doing fucking ANYTHING! "

"Ray Apt, unleashed and unchained. That is a scary thought."

"Fuck you, jagoff. So, finally my case goes to trial and the charges are dropped for a lack of evidence. I never admitted to it because the chances of them GETTIN a confession outta me was between Zero and Fuh Gettabout it. You know how a cobra holds its kill?"

"I'd imagine, tight."

"You got it, tight. And that's how you keep your secrets or the next thing you know, you're the one who's dead. I had a buddy with this huge marlin mounted on his basement wall. Only this one had a plaque on it. You know what it said?"

"I can't even begin to guess."

"It fucking said, 'If I'd kept my big mouth shut, I wouldn't be here right now.' Pretty fuckin funny, but also pretty fuckin true."

Leaning down and putting his face closer to mine,

"You know how many people there are that ain't breathin anymore cuz they met me?"

"I can't even begin to imagine Ray, nor do I want to."

I glanced over at Ray's son who was just sitting there with a stunned look on his face and his mouth was open.

"There's two rules in the Outfit and if you don't remember either of them, you're dead. Dead like Sam Giancana and Manny Skar. The first rule is, hear no evil, see no evil and keep your fucking mouth shut. The second rule is, you cheat, lie, go back on a promise, or squeal, you're also dead. No fuckin way was a confession gonna happen. On top of that, they only had what was left of the fuckin bookie plus the shotgun had no prints on it. Did I mention they also had no witnesses? Even if someone did see me, they sure as hell ain't gonna say so."

Ray takes a sip from his drink.

"Hey, here's a good one for you. Yo know why Italians got short necks?"

No, why?"

"From standing in front of a grand jury shrugging their shoulders saying 'I don't know' all the time."

"Good one, dad."

Ray takes another sip from his rum and coke and continues.

"Now I'm back out on the street and they put me to work loan sharking. I'd go see a guy who needs money and hand him $100.00. I'd tell him I'd see him next week. Next week I tell him to give me $20, but he still owes me the $100.00. The next week, it's the same drill. Only, it ain't $100 we're talking about. It's 5 G's, 10 Gs or 20 Gs! And it fuckin goes on forever cuz they never pay off the principal."

Ray sets a match to a cigarette and blows the smoke my way.

"They also had me standing at night clubs collecting cover charges. All that money goes directly to the mob. The club never sees it. And when some schmuck stepped outta line, I'd punch him out, usually break his nose and toss him in the dumpster."

"Dumb question, perhaps, but do you enjoy inflicting pain on people?"

"It ain't the pain, it's the suffering."

"Explain."

"Pain is just intense sensation. Pain becomes suffering when you add fear to it."

"Go on."

"So. you slice your finger while you're cutting up a bunch of vegetables. That's pain. Now think about me holding your hand down with my left hand while keeping your fingers spread, and I raise a sharp axe that's in my right hand with you knowing full well that I intend to chop off a finger or two, or three. Now that's suffering."

"Oh, shit."

Ya know, I told you my old man," Ray looks at his son, "your grandfather, was a violent alcoholic which is probably why he tossed me into the wall face first when I was two. What really surprised me about him years later is that he actually apologized to me and said he loved me like it was gonna change anything. I never held all that crap against him. I just knew that that sonofabitch never gave me nothing in life. And I'm sure that goes for all five of my siblings and my mom. Not love, not encouragement, not money, not nothing. Fuck, I even paid for the cocksucker's funeral. "

Ray pauses, takes another sip from his drink, and says,"You wanna talk about when Tarpey had me kidnap him?"

"Tarpey, as in Tom Tarpey, the police chief and mayor of River Grove?"

"One and the same, but he was police chief, first. Mayor came later."

"You're telling me YOU were involved and working for Tarpey? No fucking way."

Ray just smiled.

"I can also explain why he dressed like the Lone Ranger whenever he was Police Chief and put flames on his squad car. Oh, and why he went to the Olympic Committee to bring the Olympics to River Grove."

When did you kidnap him?

"When Tarpey was just starting to run for Mayor. Actually, he came to me because he knew I was working for the mob."

• CHAPTER NINE •

It was late afternoon on a Saturday when Chief Tarpey pulled up in front of White's with party lights a blazing atop his patrol car.

"What in the hell? I didn't call the cops. Who called the cops?"

"Earl, do you really think anyone in here would call the cops?"

"Good point Mac."

Tarpey looked like a man on a mission when he threw open the front door and barged in.

"Where's Ray?"

"Who?"

"Fuck you, Earl. Where's Ray?"

"Right here, Chief." The voice belonged to Apt.

"You know what Ray, we need to talk about some guy named Radtke."

"Ok by me since I don't know what the fuck you're talking about."

"Let's start by you and me going for a ride in my car."

"You're not serious."

"As serious as a heart attack."

"You're a bigger asshole than I ever imagined. Ok, let's go."

Ray left a fiver on the bar before leaving with Tarpey.

"I'll hold your change, Ray."

"Don't bother, Earl. Buy yourself a cocktail."

The two men got into the squad car.

"Wow. You came alone. Sure you can handle me alone?"

"Knock off the shit, Ray. I need your help."

Ray sat expressionless, yet silent as Tarpey threw the car into drive and sped off down Grand Avenue heading west.

"Number one, jagoff, I know damn well it was you who beat the fuck outta that guy Radtke because only you could bust a guy up like that and leave him with a broken nose. Number two, I could care less. Schiller Park called me in on it and I told 'em I'd check into it. Ok, consider it checked into. Number three, I'm fuckin in trouble and need your help."

Ray remained expressionless and silent.

"You know I'm running for Mayor."

Ray nodded, said nothing, but smiled.

"What's the smile for?"

"You do know that Bill Ott is running for Town Clerk."

"With his record? Really? He hasn't got a chance."

"I think he has a great campaign slogan."

"Like what?"

"Why Not Ott?!?"

"Oh, brother. I can give you a couple hundred reasons why not Ott. He hasn't got a chance."

"And you?"

"Well, there are a lot of people around who would rather I didn't run because I DO have a chance. People like Mayor Wolf, Harry Steigerwaldt, Sr., Jim Kirie, and your employers in River Forest."

"Tom, I think if my employers didn't want you running for Mayor, I'd of fuckin heard about it and you'd be a non-breather right now."

Tarpey pulled the squad car into the parking lot of Dominick's shopping center, brought it to an abrupt stop, slammed it into park and shut off the motor.

"Ray, you remember when Judge Boyle, who didn't even have a law degree, became mayor, O'Hallen was police chief and Elmer Conti ran Elmwood Park?"

Ray nodded yes.

"Well, during that time, your former employers, Accardo, Giancana, and Manny Skar owned and operated both Elmwood Park and River Grove through Conti. Boyle was just a yes man for Conti and O'Hallen was the enforcer."

"So, what? They also owned Melrose Park, Stone Park, Oak Park, Rosemont, Schiller Park, Franklin Park, and Glitter Gulch on the Mannheim strip and every fucking thing within a hundred-mile radius."

"Exactly."

"Tom, I get it. But so what?"

"So what is that Boyle was replaced by a more reliable and connected Elmer Wolf. O'Hallen finally got old and retired. Conti remained Mayor of Elmwood Park and only became more and more powerful. Eventually, River Forest got tired of fuckin around with River Grove because it wasn't worth the effort. That was until Steigerwaldt Realty opened up here last spring. You do know who Harry Steigerwaldt, Sr. is?"

"Yeh. The mouthpiece for, as you say, my employers. I've met him and his kid."

"Well, he and junior have opened up this realty company down the street from Whites."

While listening, Apt set fire to a Marlboro.

"You ever meet Jim Kirie?"

"Sure. He owns Kirie's restaurant on the corner by the tracks on Thatcher across from Quastoff's and south of the cemetery."

"Right. And he's also the President of the School Board."

"Tom, I'm sitting in your fucking car at one o'clock in the afternoon so you can give me a civics lesson and tell me about old man Kirie. What the fuck?"

"You want to help me or not?"

"I never said I wanted to help you. You just came to White's and grabbed me, remember?"

"You know, as Mary said to Joseph, so who the fuck needs you? Sorry I wasted your time."

Ray, who could read people very well, saw genuine fear in Tarpey.

"Wow, Tom. You really are shook. Ok, I'll shut up. You just keep talking. So, what's with Kirie?:

Now Tarpey lit a cigarette and inhaled deeply.

"He's on Steigerwaldt's payroll. Steigerwaldt just bought up all the land surrounding the school, plus all the land on the northeast part of town, plus he has a 65 percent interest in the Thirsty Whale."

"Pretend I'm dumb. What's all that add up to?"

"It adds up to Harry Steigerwaldt making a play to take back River Grove and make a lotta money for all the wrong reasons. With Kirie running the school board, he'll push through a bond issue to buy up the property surrounding the school that Steigerwaldt now owns. And the reason that's gonna happen is because River Grove, for whatever reason, is rapidly growing in population and will need a bigger school. Also, as Building Commissioner, Kirie will push for a large new shopping center and apartment complex in the northeast part of town on the very same land that Steigerwaldt also owns. Plus, the Thirsty Whale is an ideal place to launder money for them."

"Ok, so Steigerwaldt comes away a millionaire. You really think that bothers my conscience?"

"The money isn't the issue. What all this adds up to is that your employers in River Forest want back into River Grove. And the only way they can really pull that off is by eliminating the one person who can get in their way."

"He'd have to clear all this with DiFronzo."

"You mean the guy who lives with his wife on Grand just west of Elmwood Park?"

"One and the same."

"Is he really that powerful?"

"He keeps a low profile."

"Wow."

"You think you're gonna get whacked?"

"Well, Steigerwaldt already tried bribing me."

"Tom, just take the fuckin money and run."

"Ray. Just how long do you think I'd have to enjoy it? Plus, my conscience is slightly larger than yours. It would eat at me and I know it."

"So, you're gonna oppose 'em, or expose them?"

"Oppose them for as long as I can, at least until I can really expose them."

"Big difference. They'll put up with being opposed. Exposure will get you killed for sure. Plus, you do know they have a long goddamn memory."

"What do you mean by that?"

"You remember that small time bookie Lou Bombacino?"

"Yeh, the guy who took on Capone?"

"No. That was Roger Touhy. Bombacino told the Feds what they wanted to know and Jackie Cerone ended up in prison because of it. But eight years later, they found the son of a bitch in Arizona and took him out."

"I see your point" said Tarpey inhaling deeply on his cigarette.

"So, what do you want from me?"

A stream of smoke was exhaled through Tarpey's nose.

"Protection."

• CHAPTER TEN •

"Can you believe that fucking Mayor Wolf and the Village Trustees held a special, unscheduled meeting to pass this new piece of bullshit so that every cop on the force, including me has to pass a psychological exam before being allowed to remain on the job."

"You know they're doing this just because you're running for mayor."

"First off, I'm gonna pass this fuckin test. Then I'm gonna call the American Civil Liberties Union and maybe Jesse Jackson for River Grove not even coming close to meeting the number of minorities that should be on both the police force and the fire department."

"Whoa! Whoa!! Whoa!!! Are you nuts?!? We haven't had a black living in River Grove since that black scientist Dr. Julien who owned Julien Labs house burned down."

"Yeh. And you know WHY his house burned down?"

"Sure. Because River Grove has a volunteer fire department and none of the volunteers showed up to put out the fire. Tom, I'm telling you, don't go there. You'd not only have the THE mob coming after you, but A mob coming after you, too."

"I thought this was the Village of Friendly Neighbors."

"It is, provided all the neighbors are White."

By late August, the mayoral campaign had grown pretty heated, with the primary election slated for Tuesday, September seventh, 1973.

But, according to the local paper, "Mayoral candidate and police chief, Tom Tarpey called published reports from a so called 'informed source' stating that he is withdrawing from the race, 'rumor and innuendo.' Rumor had it that Tarpey would not run because he needed to devote more time to his job as police chief and to his family."

"Do you believe this crap? Like I'm gonna drop out now. Plus, I don't even have a family! I have a wife. No kids. Where do they come up with this stuff?"

"I like this other story better."

"What story."

63

"The paper previously reported that Bill Ott, a convicted felon now running for town clerk had one time been arrested by the Cook County Sheriff's department for possession of 30 pounds of marijuana. Ott demanded a retraction saying he wouldn't be caught dead with thirty pounds of marijuana and that the actual number was THREE HUNDRED POUNDS and to get the story straight!"

"Only Bill would do that."

"Hey! Why not Ott?"

"Exactly!"

On September seventh, twenty-five percent of the eligible voters turned out to vote for Tom Tarpey as their candidate on the Village Party ticket for mayor. Of the 11,389 votes tallied, Tarpey had well over 8,000 votes. Bill Ott amassed seven votes.

"I think they're feeling some pressure now that they know you'll be running against them, which means they're gonna do something and soon."

And that they did. "The Village Trustees, Tuesday, voted to do away with residential zoning on two downtown properties adjacent to the areas growing commercial center. The trustees unanimously changed the zoning of the property located across from the proposed regional shopping center from R4 residential to C-2 commercial," as was reported by the Village News.

"Well, they're certainly upping the ante and the pressure."

"Yeh, it also means they can't afford to have me win the election."

"So, what precautions are you taking?"

"I already sent Alice back to Indiana to stay with her parents. And I hired a bodyguard."

"Who? Sergeant Odo?"

"No. Ray Apt."

Tom's brother Bob just stared at him in stark disbelief.

"You know NOBODY, but NOBODY can know you have Ray Apt working for you. Oh, my god they'd have a field day with that. What if Apt talks?"

"You ever talk to Ray Apt?"

"No. I never actually met him. Only know him by reputation."

"Well, I can assure you that talking is NOT one of Ray's strong suits."

Bob Tarpey, Tom's older brother, like Tom, had grown up and settled in the Village of River Grove. Unlike Tom, Bob married young and divorced his first wife after a great many heated arguments and a plethora of 'un-reconcilable differences.' Bob was quite content with his life, including his second marriage, and being the campaign manager for his brother. But he certainly wasn't comfortable knowing Ray Apt was now his brother's protector.

"Are you seriously afraid that you're gonna get bumped off?"

"As serious as a stroke. Look Bob, you aren't exactly the safest person in the world right now, either."

"Why, because the hitman may miss you and hit me instead?"

The following week, Bob Tarpey found out firsthand just how safe he was when the Wolf campaign committee mailed out their first campaign mailer that completely ignored his brother and instead attacked Bob.

The mailer, a one-page, one-sided flyer, folded in three parts was mailed to all the registered voters in the Village. It pointed out Bob's arrest for assaulting his first wife during a domestic dispute back in 1962, for which he paid a $75.00 fine.

"How do they get hold of a confidential police record on a case that is well over ten years old? Not only is this bullshit, but why are they coming after me?!?"

"Because you're my brother and campaign manager."

"You know what I'm gonna do?"

"Yes. Nothing. Just settle down. They want you to overreact."

"Settle down?!? You kidding? Wait till my wife starts yelling at me and wondering how I could have been such an asshole as to beat my wife... and then she's gonna start looking at me funny like I'm gonna beat her up next."

The next day the Village News reported:

"FIRE FIGHTERS ENDORSE CHALLENGER TARPEY
The Fire Fighters Association, Tuesday, endorsed Thomas J. Tarpey by majority vote. The decision was then ratified by the association's board of directors at a 7:30pm meeting. This now makes it unanimous for Tarpey in that the Police Officers Association, and the International Brotherhood of Electrical Workers have all voted to support him. Tarpey said he hopes the union's endorsements carry some weight in the upcoming election.

When asked about the felony and misdemeanor stories recently disclosed in a campaign flyer sent out by the opposition, the Chief of Police responded, 'No Comment.'"

"Well, at least we have the unions behind us.'

"Christ, I wish I had my wife behind me. She's still looking at me funny."

Election day was but a month away.

As reported in the Village News:

"MAYOR RECEIVES DEATH THREAT
An air of uneasiness may settle on the Trustees Meeting tonight when it meets to discuss a zone change.

Someone has threatened to kill the mayor should the proposed zone change be approved, the mayor said in a press conference.

"The letter came in the form of a plain wrapper and threatened to kill me and all the Trustees. It's been quite a while since I've gotten one of these, but over the years I've had three or four.'

"The letter, written in rhyme, was sent over two weeks ago. Along with the note was a chopped-up copy of the public notice announcing the proposed zoning change.

"It adds a little spice to the program,' the Mayor quipped, but added, 'It is kind of scary because

it involves more than just me.'

"'In the twenty-two years I've been on the force, there has been maybe a half dozen of these kinds of threats,' said Chief Tarpey. "Nothing ever became of any of them. Just in case, though, we'll have extra men at tonight's meeting."

The meeting started promptly at 7:30pm just after the Pledge of Allegiance was said.

"Any new business?"

"Yes, your honor. I'd like to propose a zone change for the 88-unit apartment building and 94-unit apartment building scheduled to be built on Lot 56 through 97, Tract 9761 through 9782 from the R-1, low multiple to an R-5 high multiple dwelling. We feel this should be done in order to provide housing for the thousands of workers who will be flocking into our town when the highrise office buildings open."

"All right, any further discussion?" Mayor Wolf waited about a nanosecond before continuing. "No? Ok, all in favor, say 'I'. Opposed? The re-zoning passes unanimously. Any more new business?

"So much for the death threat."

• CHAPTER ELEVEN •

On Tuesday, November seventh, Election Day, the voters turned out in droves. The election not only generated the highest voter turnout in the history of the Village, but it was also the tightest. With 21 precincts reporting, Tarpey trailed Wolf by two percent. After counting some 5,368 ballots though, Tarpey took a slim lead. It was an edge that held until Wolf crept back ahead with fifty-seven precincts reporting. It was Wolf with 6,336 votes to Tarpey's 6,287. When it was all over, Tarpey had bested Wolf for the win with 9,646 votes to 9,544 and became River Grove's new Mayor.

"Jesus H. Christ on a crutch, we did it!! We really did it!"

"Fuckin A man, I don't believe it. Talk about luck!"

"Luck, nuthin! You were a shoe in to win!'

"What in the fuck are you two derelicts so jubilant about" Earl inquired of Rick and Terry Raffin.

"Terry here just got elected Lieutenant of the Service Repairman's Union for Maytag!"

"Christ, here I thought you were all jazzed over Tarpey beating out Wolf for Mayor."

"He did?!?"

"Yeh. Won it by a whisker."

"I'll be damned. Guess there goes my shot at getting in the reserves."

"How's that?"

"I was thinking of becoming a part time reserve cop for Tarpey, but I guess he ain't gonna be Chief anymore."

"Guess wrong. He announced he's gonna hold both jobs."

"I'll drink to that! Make it another Old Style!!"

"I think maybe you should find Tarpey and congratulate him. It may improve your chances."

"Good idea, Earl!"

As Village Mayor, Tom Tarpey called for a six month moratorium on the issuance of all building permits. The public hearing that ensued was held at the auditorium of the public grade school. The very school that Steigerwaldt, Sr. and company had their eye on. Tarpey, in an attempt to forestall, if not thwart the bond issue that Jim Kirie and Steigerwaldt would push for, came up with the idea for a moratorium. To say Steigerwaldt was exacerbated would be putting it mildly,

"Just who in the fuck does that asshole think he is with this moratorium bullshit? That's it. That fucker's gotta go. We gotta get all the realtors and contractors together to fight this one."

And that they did. The hearing was attended by over 1000 residents. Some 300 plus wore colored tags identifying themselves as residents, realtors, merchants and homeowners who had signed petitions against the moratorium.

"Look. The Board of Trustees and the Planning Committee have had more than sufficient controls on development. All this moratorium is going to do is frighten investors and keep corporations from coming here."

When it became apparent that Tarpey had insufficient support to pass the ordinance, he addressed the forum crowd: "Well, at least this meeting proves that the Trustees care about planning and that we wanted to hear community opinions. At least this hearing has helped restore the Trustees' and the Village Staff's credibility."

"That's right," chimed in V. John Saari, Tarpey's lone supporter. "We're here to protect you and the developers in this community. If it scares away developers by saying give me ninety days, then it's possible they are working with blinders on."

Mr. Butch Woodrum, speaking for the Village Chamber of Commerce then came up with an idea. "What we oughta do is form a land use commission comprised of residents, members of the chamber, and the board of Trustees. Then give them a set period of time to study issues and provide input to the Village."

"I think that's a wonderful idea, Mr. Woodrum," Mayor Tarpey concurred, knowing full well it would also work to forestall Steigerwaldt, who was becoming angrier with each passing minute.

"I think there is a limit to how much growth our town can handle... half a plan is better than no plan at all. And, while you're at it, put a limit on how high a building can be when it's near a residential area."

Community Development Director, Jim Rabjohn then jumped in. "We need time to draw a blueprint for this town's future so that only those projects appropriate to the area would be approved."

Then it was Harry Steigerwaldt, Sr.'s turn who was a whole lot more red in the face than somewhat. "C'mon. Let's get on with it. I say let's vote on creating a Village Economic Council. It's charter to be to conduct a nationwide campaign to convince businesses to relocate here. Then, we must vote on who will sit on the council. I personally agree with Mr. Woodrum and have it consist of residents, members of the chamber and the Board of Trustees.

"Is that a motion, Mr. Steigerwaldt?"

"Damn well right it is."

"I second it," cried out Jim Kirie.

"All right then, let's vote on it."

"WHOA, WHOA, WHOA! What in the hell do you think is going on here?!? A red faced, angry Mayor Tarpey yelled while banging his gavel.

"A vote!" Snapped back Steigerwaldt.

"A vote my butt! I'm the Mayor and I'm the head of this council Mr. Steigerwaldt and I will not be intimidated by your trying to railroad this meeting and the procedures. I'll be the one to take the roll and I will be the one to call for a vote. Have I made myself perfectly clear to you Mr. Steigerwaldt? If I haven't, I 'd be glad to have you escorted out of here."

Harry Steigerwaldt, turning an even brighter red, refused to answer.

"Mr. Steigerwaldt, I will ask you again. Do you understand me?"

With an urge to kill, Steigerwaldt finally answered, "Yes."

"All right. Now that we have that settled, I move the previous question."

"And I second it," jumped in Mr. Saari.

"Just what in the hell does that mean, Mr. Mayor?"

"According to Robert's Rule of Order, it means we will vote to see if we want to vote on it."

"Jesus Christ, this could take all night!"

"Mr. Kirie, I am prepared to stay here until Hell freezes over if I have to in order that this forum accomplishes everything it has set out to do here this evening. And let me make myself perfectly clear when I say that there will be no motions railroaded through here tonight or rammed down anyone's throat."

After close to two hours of debate and roll calling, the forum had decided that it was prepared to vote on having a council made up of residents, members of the chamber and the board of trustees, but would take nominations and vote on them later.

"Now how many people do you wish to have on this council?"

"As many as it takes!"

"That's not a number."

"No more than ten!"

"I say at least twenty!"

The four-hour public forum finally came to a close after hour number five. It never did produce the moratorium Tarpey had hoped for, but it certainly did forestall Harry Steigerwaldt, Sr. and his coterie from ramming his programs through a handpicked "blue ribbon" council. The final act of the evening came when those remaining voted to create a nine-person, economic council that would study the issues and provide input to the Board of Trustees. They would be allowed to try and convince corporations to move into the Village on a nationwide basis. All told, Tarpey won this evening's battle, which was evident by Harry Steigerwaldt's storming out of the school auditorium, with Jim Kirie running right behind him.

"C'mon, Kirie! I need a drink!! We're going back to my office. I gotta make a phone call."

Both men hopped into Steigerwaldt's Fleetwood Cadillac and sped off as Tarpey watched them go.

Steigerwaldt swiftly opened the door to his realty office located a mere six blocks from the grade school.

"The booze is in the cabinet. Pour me four fingers of Chivas on the rocks. Help yourself to whatever you're drinking. I gotta make this phone call."

Harry angrily snatched up the telephone and punched out seven buttons. "Hello, Marty?" Yeh. Yeh. Say, what the fuck happened to our boys? Yeh. Hell, no!! The fucking asshole is still strutting around like he owns the place. No, I don't know what happened to them. That's why I'm calling YOU! Oh, shit. Really? Both of them?!? Jesus Christ, what kind of amateurs are we hiring these days? No, I don't care. Look, Tarpey's gotta go and that's all there is to it. No! We can't wait much longer. C'mon we both know the timetable he gave us and we're gonna stick to it. Big fucking deal!! Up yours, Marty! I did my part, now go do yours. Yeh. Right!! Say Hi to Rosalie and the kids for me. Bye."

Turning back to Kirie. "Jesus H. Christ, that Tarpey bugs me. How that piece of shit ever won the election is beyond me."

"Calm down, Harry. Drink this and sit down. We won tonight."

"Your ass we won!"

Steigerwaldt drained the four fingers of Chivas and sat down. "God, that jagoff pisses me off. But hopefully, for not much longer."

• CHAPTER TWELVE •

"Ok, little brother. I have devised a plan to keep you alive."

"You're going to hire Ray Apt's twin brother?"

"No. But Apt does come to play in this plan. We gotta get you statewide, if not nationwide publicity."

"Bob, I'm a chief of police and mayor for a small village in the Chicagoland suburbs. Who's gonna care? I'm small potatoes."

"Until you're not. Remember that Texas Judge named Roy Bean who was actually a self-declared judge just because he'd come across a law book?"

"Vaguely."

"Well, the man was full-goose, bozo nuts! But it made him a legend. He did every off the wall thing imaginable and because of it had books and movies telling his story."

"So, you want me to be full goose bozo nuts?"

"Not necessarily, but I do want you to do some very off the wall stuff?"

"Like?"

"Like how you dress and the car you drive."

"What's wrong with either?"

"Nothing, other than that they're too plain, too conservative and too unnoticeable. I want you dressing and looking like the Lone Ranger, minus the mask, but the hat is optional. Secondly, you're gonna have flames painted on your squad car."

"People will think I'm nuts."

"Exactly! We not only want people to think you're nuts, but we want you to stand out in a crowd and be noticed, because I'm gonna run a PR campaign on you to get your name in every newspaper in the state of Illinois and hopefully the country. The mob can't bump you off without fear of a thorough investigation if everyone knows who you are."

Tom, looking quite skeptical asks, "Bob, you mentioned Apt before. So, what role do you have him play in this scheme of yours, Tonto?"

"No. A while back you told me about the first conversation you had with Ray in your car and how you brought up Roger the Terrible Touhy while Apt was talking about the guy bumped off in Arizona. So, I looked into Roger the Terrible Touhy. You know what Touhy got sent up for?"

"No."

"He got sent up for kidnapping Joe the Barber to keep him from getting deported back to England. It wasn't a real kidnapping, it was just a way to hide. So Apt is gonna kidnap you shortly after he beats the crap out of you in front of everyone."

"You're looney."

"No, I'm not but you're sure gonna be. Look, everyone knows Ray's reputation. He gets in a fight with you and shortly after that you disappear. Who they gonna think made you disappear? Most people, like Steigerwaldt, will figure you for dead. But instead, you'll just be hiding out in Wisconsin somewhere for a week or two."

"What does that buy us?"

"It buys you time and lowers the chances of you becoming a non-breather anytime soon. Plus, it will make Steigerwaldt overly confident."

"And?"

"And by being overly confident, he's gonna make a mistake."

"You got this all figured out, hunh."

"I do and have been giving this a lot of thought for quite some time."

"What's the order of events?"

"I already bought you your new uniform. It comes with a white hat, but as I said, that's optional."

"You're joking."

"No, I'm not, because here it is." Bob hands Tom the box. "Oh, and here are the boots that go with it, just your size."

"This is crazy."

"Exactly!"

"And my car?"

"Should be out of the shop today."

"What?!? You already had the flames painted on?!?!"

"Yeh, and it's spectacular!!"

Tom sits down. "Bob, I don't know about this."

"Tom, you just have to trust me on this. It's gonna save your life and probably mine, too."

"And when does Apt kidnap me?"

"After he beats you up."

"And when is that?"

"In about two weeks after people get used to you in the new Outfit and car."

"So, the Lone Ranger loses?"

"Oh, no! The Lone Ranger never loses. He pretty much got beaten up every episode but always won in the end... just like you're gonna do."

Reluctantly, Mayor/Chief of Police Tarpey wore the uniform, hat included and drove his newly painted squad car with flames all over the hood and front fenders.

• CHAPTER THIRTEEN •

For the village trustees to hold more than a shot glass, cigarette and a handful of cards was really news in River Grove. Which explains the headline in the local River Grove Messenger newspaper... *"Village Trustees Hold Special Meeting."* The article read, *"a special meeting of the Village Board of Trustees was called to order at 7:30pm, Thursday, with Mayor Tom Tarpey presiding. As Village Mayor, Police Chief and Liquor Commissioner, he reported on the following taverns: Villa Rose Pizzeria has been sold and will become the Italian Village having applied for a new license. White's Tavern has also been sold; The Deer Head is under new management."*

"Otto, who the fuck's that?"

"The new Earl."

"Looks like Marge finally wore Earl down, hunh?"

"Yeh, women have a way of doing that."

"Sad he never said a word and never said goodbye."

"What can I tell you? Impermanence is a fact of life and we all gotta get used to it."

The new Earl was a tough, stocky Italian broad named Betty Corrigan who made her money as a hair stylist working for Sassoon, then Paul Mitchell in Chicago's Gold Coast. About five two, 126 pounds stuffed into an Outfit that was a size or two too small for her and wreaking of perfume. Plus, she had a voice not to dissimilar from that of Wallace Beery.

"You get a whiff of that perfume?"

"Yeh. Smells like Midnight in Berwyn."

"Ya know, I think I'm gonna fix this place up and make it more upscale."

Bill's eyes went up into his head and said, "You gotta be kiddin?"

"No. I'm gonna make it more Disco." With that Bill spit out his beer in disbelief.

"You fuckin slob! Ain't ya got no class at all?"

"Lady, all I can say is you're outta your fuckin head."

"Back off, sweetheart. I'll keep the name the same, but this interior's gotta go."

"Are you nuts? You know who comes in here? You're gonna invest good coin to fix this dump up just so DT and the Sorenson twins can puke and pass out on the bar? I'm tellin ya lady, the same crowd's gonna show up whether it looks like it does now or has a disco ball and sexy red lights. Why bother?"

"Look, pal, whoever you are."

"I'm Bill."

"Ok, Bill. It's my money and I'll do what I damn well want with the place. Got it?"

"Got it. But if you take that rotating Schlitz clock down I'll buy it from you."

"Why would you want that?"

"As a reminder of the old White's Tavern before you fucked it up."

• CHAPTER FOURTEEN •

Thanksgiving Day in the Tavern always held a dichotomy of emotions. On the one hand, it appeared sad and depressing. On the other, it was uniquely heartwarming to witness. Betty, like Earl before her, carried on the tradition by providing turkey and all the trimmings for the regular patrons who either had nowhere else to go, or were seeking refuge from their families.

"You guys ever consider what day this is and the thought of maybe being thankful for something?"

"Sure. I'm thankful White's is open!"

"Jesus."

"Aw, Betty. We're just practicing for Christmas."

"Well, I can't wait to see what in the hell that's gonna be like."

"Hey, Macatelli, you know what you're getting for Christmas this year?"

"Yeh. Same thing I got last year. Drunk."

"Elaine, you know who I saw last week?"

"Let me guess. Your shadow."

"No, Fat Joe. They let him out early for good behavior."

"I didn't even know he was in again."

"Yeh, he got five years for seventeen counts of check forgeries in four counties."

"Ok, the turkey should be out in about another hour."

"Maybe DT will be awake by then."

"It ain't even half time, yet."

"From the way he smells, I think he was wearing last night's booze as this morning's cologne."

"Betty, give 'em a break. He had a half pint of vodka for breakfast this morning."

"Throw a blanket on him, for Crissakes."

Betty barely got the last word out of her mouth when her eyes went as wide as the front door opening. Walking through it was none other than Police Chief Tarpey in his new Lone Ranger Outfit."

Regaining her composure, Betty quipped, "Obviously you ain't playing Mayor today. What in the hell brings you in here on Thanksgiving?"

It was seldom if ever Tom Tarpey visited White's Tavern just to say hello, so the question going through everyone's mind was, 'what happened to who and who did what?'

"Well, Mayor Tom, I mean Chief, Happy Thanksgiving. It's good to see you." said Brian King nonchalantly, while holding his usual five grams of coke.

"Happy Thanksgiving to you, too Brian. And to everyone! Actually, Betty, I'm glad you're carrying on Earl's tradition to feed these maniacs."

"Yeh, I figured I ain't got anywhere to go myself, so why not? And to what do we owe the honor of your company? You gotta have a better place to be today than here. "

"Truthfully, I'm here looking for Raymond."

"You can see for yourself, he ain't here and I haven't seen him yet today."

"Anyway, if you see him, let him know I need to talk to him."

Tarpey turned toward the door to go and looked up at the small, black and white portable television Betty had stuck atop the Juke box, "How're the Bears doing?"

"Tied score, three to three."

"Take care, folks."

"Bye, Chief!"

And with that Chief Tarpey exited White's Tavern.

"What the fuck!?! I can't believe he just came in here like that!"

"Me, neither. I think I got some skid marks on my shorts."

"Hey! Tarpey's Okay. Wotchya sweating about? Like he said, he's just looking for Ray."

"That's it", said Betty. This week I'm putting up Christmas decorations and making this place a little homier and a lot more festive."

"Shit!"

"What?!?"

"The Lions just scored on the Bears."

"You know, Holidays are just tough on us all."

"Can I have another Old Style?"

"Isn't that turkey done, yet?"

That night, the Chief's flame engulfed squad car was parked in a cold, dark alley. Inside was Chief Tarpey and Ray Apt.

"I gotta hand it to you, Chief. You have everyone thinking you're looking to haul my ass in jail."

"I am!" Tarpey said jokingly. "Ya know, I thought Macatelli was gonna shit in his drawers when he saw me walking in."

"Ok, so you found me and I'm here. Now what?"

"You know who those two guys were that you made disappear the other night?"

"I haven't the faintest idea what in the fuck you're talking about."

"Well first off, thank you for taking care of those two guys you know nothing about and never saw. Secondly, I found out Harry Steigerwaldt hired them to make me deader than last Tuesday. And that was in spite of me wearing this Outfit, the car with flames and my brother's public relations campaign on me."

"Hell, your brother even got you a story and a picture in the Trib."

"And they still want to bump me off. I don't know what more I can do."

"Remember when you threatened Wolf with going to the ACLU because there were no blacks on the force or on the fire department? Well, fuckin go through with it. If they bumped you off then, you can bet your ass there'd not only be a federal investigation that wouldn't quit, but River Grove would have Jesse Jackson down its throat."

"Oh, great. Now you want me dying for a cause."

"You're not listening, Tom. They're not about to kill you if they know the Feds and the NAACP are gonna be all over this town like white on rice. One of the townies may take a shot at you, but it won't be a professional."

"Oh, now that's comforting."

"Hey, I thought your brother was going to have you contact the Olympic Committee to have the Olympics come to River Grove?"

"We did. We're just waiting to hear back. Can you imagine what the press is gonna do with a gun toting, mayor and police chief who dresses like the Lone Ranger and drives a flame covered squad car asking the Olympic Committee to consider holding the Olympics in River Grove?"

"Tom, you're gonna get National attention with that one and be more famous than Gene and Jude's. You'll be too famous to kill."

"Hey, Marilyn Monroe was about as famous as you can get."

"And so was Julius Caesar. Only, you ain't either of those people."

"Ray, I gotta get back to the station. Thanks again for taking care of those two guys you know nothing about and saving my ass. You got anything else to add?"

"Yeh, Ricky Raffin wants to get on the reserves."

"He's already approached me about that."

"Well, make sure he gets on soon."

"Is Rick working with you?"

"No, not yet. He doesn't know anything about nothing yet. But I may need him and his being a cop would help."

"I'll put him on tomorrow."

Promptly at 7:30pm on the Tuesday after Thanksgiving, Mayor Tom Tarpey opened the Board of Trustees meeting to nominate people for the Blue Ribbon Economic Council.

"We will accept nominations only tonight. No voting will take place. Keep in mind there are only nine seats open this council. So please, nominate only someone you think will do a very good job, will do what's best for the Village, and is very serious about being on this advisory council." Tom clears his throat. "At the next meeting to be held one week from tonight, we will vote on the nominees and create the economics council. Then, as a group, the members of this council will create a written charter for the council to follow. Everyone on board with all of this?"

"Why can't we just nominate and vote on them tonight?"

"Because this is a very serious matter and I want everyone to just go home and think about the nominees for a week, then determine who you think would be the best person or should I say, persons for the job."

After some grumbling, the Mayor continued. "Now, as we agreed at last week's meeting, the council will consist of residents and members of the Chamber of Commerce, only. Neither developers or contractors with on-going projects in the area, or relatives of those developers and contractors be allowed to serve on the council."

"You can't do that! That's nuts!"

"I just don't want to see anyone on this council who has a shot at personal gain. And I don't want any council member coercing fellow council members and swaying decisions. We want to do what's right and what's best for River Grove and not what's best for some individual."

"Wait a minute, now. I thought this council was supposed to be made up of a cross section of interests. Relatives of contractors and developers are first and foremost residents and have every right to be on this council. You can't just arbitrarily rule they can't be nominated."

Tarpey, now frustrated, "OK! Ok! Let's forget the relatives and just keep it to no contractors and no developers."

"Fine!"

Some two agonizingly long hours later, there were twenty-eight people nominated for the nine seats available.

• CHAPTER FIFTEEN •

David Jessen was the Village District Attorney and a close personal friend of both Tom and Bob Tarpey.

"Tom, I think I've added another fly to Steigerwaldt's ointment."

"What're you talking about, David?"

"We nailed one of Steigerwaldt's major nominees just in time for Thursday's meeting."

"Which one?"

"Enger."

"How?"

"I had Tom Conrad ask that Enger's name be taken off the nominee list because Tom was getting a lot of phone calls about Enger's ties to Harry Steigerwaldt."

"You're losing me here. We can't just take him off the list because he hangs out with Harry."

"No. But we can when I prove that Marty Enger is a silent partner in a lot of these Harry Steigerwaldt owned development projects. Enger never used his name, just his money."

"Why wasn't this addressed at the nominating meeting and why is it all suddenly surfacing now?"

"Easy. I didn't have enough information on Enger to nail him at the meeting, but I do now. I followed Enger's money trail and it led right to Harry. Then I let Conrad know about it and I'm sure he's already informed Enger."

"What you think Enger will do now?"

"He's doing it already. He announced he's holding a press conference late today."

"You think he's going to announce his withdrawal?"

"Not if Harry Steigerwaldt, Sr. has anything to say about it."

Late that afternoon, Martin Enger held his press conference and told those attending that, "All I care about is that River Grove remain River Grove. That this village is very much a single-family environment and should remain that way, although I am not here to defend any position. I do favor planned growth, but I certainly have no idea where the criticism of my nomination came from. My company is not involved in any project in River Grove and never has. And, no offense to the Village, but I have to add that not one piece of property in River Grove would be of interest to a company the magnitude of mine. Therefore, I am NOT withdrawing my name from nomination for the following two reasons. One, I have no projects going on here in River Grove. And two, it is only a nomination. I have not won the seat, so why all the ruckus? I say let the voters decide on Tuesday night."

On Tuesday night, the public meeting was once again held in the public grade school's auditorium.

"Good evening ladies and gentlemen. Because of the rather large turn out, we have decided to forego with a verbal vote and use ballot instead. Hopefully, you received your ballot at the door when you walked in. If you did not, please notify one of the ushers and they will see to it that you get one."

"How many ballots do we each get?"

"Just one, thank you. Just one. We may be in Cook County, but we're River Grove and not Chicago."

"What happened to vote early and vote often?

"That's still Chicago, not us. And if you see someone with two ballots, please point them out. This needs to be a fair and honest election."

"What're we supposed to do with the ballots after we fill them out?"

"As you see, there are no voting booths. So, mark your ballot at your seat, fold it in half when you're done and raise your hand. An usher will come by to take your ballot and deposit it into these boxes each usher will be holding." Tom holds up a ballot box for everyone to see.

"All the ballots will be collected and counted by the very same election committee that counts the ballots in every election. The results will then be tabulated and posted by no later than Friday morning at ten am, at which time a press conference will be held to announce the winners. Good luck to all."

Less than ninety minutes later the auditorium had emptied out as the last vote was now cast.

Bob Tarpey approached his brother Tom.

"Before I tell you what I think, what do you think?"

"I think Harry Steigerwaldt, Sr. is going to win with Marty Novelli and Marty Enger. God, I wish we could've gotten Enger off the ballot."

"David sure tried."

"I also think that with those two on the council, plus Wolf's Board of Trustees, it's gonna be one helluvan uphill battle for us."

"Unfortunately, I see it the same way you do."

"C'mon, brother Bob, I need a drink."

"You mind if I don't join you? Believe it or not, my wife is finally starting to trust me again after Wolf pulled that shit about me being a wife beater. I think I'd be better off going home."

"No, I don't mind and am happy to hear it! As a matter of fact, I think I'm going to go find Apt and touch base with him."

"You ok with him?"

"What choice do I have?"

"None."

"Raymond?!?"

Ray had been hanging back in the darkness waiting for the two men to part.

"Jesus H. Christ, do you always have to sneak up on people?"

"Look Tom, if I were one of Steigerwaldt's guys, you'd be dead right now."

"That's comforting."

"You want to stay alive or what?"

"Well, if you give me a heart attack, it ain't gonna matter no how, now is it?"

"I just figured it was time we touched base again."

"You figured right because I was about to go over to White's Tavern to see what I could pin on you this time," Tom said smiling.

"So, bring me up to speed."

"I'm figuring that if Enger and Novelli both get on that council, I'm far less of a threat. But, if they don't get on, I could be dead meat. Truthfully, I'm hoping I'm dead meat because I really don't want those two on that council. It would be game over for River Grove."

"You do know I could care less what happens to River Grove. My only concern is keeping you alive. Glad you got Raffin on the reserves because it looks like I'm gonna need him."

"Why don't we wait till the results are in?"

"No fucking way. I'd rather I have him with me before I need him than scramble to bring him on board when it may be too late."

"Were you at tonight's meeting?"

"Hell, no. I just slipped in when everyone was leaving. By the way, quit walking around by yourself, even a short distance."

"Thanks, Ray. After your little exhibition of stealth just now, trust me, I learned.... Now where in the fuck did he go?"

Ray Apt, the shape shifter disappeared into the darkness.

"What a strange guy," Tarpey thought to himself. "And, oh shit, here I am alone again," he continued the thought and quickly jumped into his squad car slamming the door behind him.

On Friday morning, the press conference to announce the winners went off as scheduled.

"Now before I announce the winners, I hope everyone elected to this committee realizes that this is an advisory board to the Trustees and just that. Secondly, the first meeting of this Blue Ribbon committee will be held this coming Tuesday at six pm before the regularly scheduled Board of Trustees meeting that begins at seven pm. "

"For Crissakes, Tom! Who in the hell won?!?"

"Glad you asked that. The resident and chamber winners to sit on the committee are the following: Mr. Wally Warchol, Mrs. Tova Bichel, Mr. Larry Cossack, Mr. Harry Eggert, Mrs. Philip Piscopo. Mr. Lerner, Mrs. Czajka, Mr. Rabjohn, and Mr. Hempel."

"What?!?!" The word belonged to a red-faced Jim Kirie who was more surprised by his outburst than anyone. The fact that he never heard the name Enger or Novelli just sort of overwhelmed him.

"Yes, Mr. Kirie, you have a question?"

"Ahhh, no. No. I'm sorry for interrupting."

"And finally, representing the Board of Trustees, we have Trustee Tom Conrad, and Trustee DeCoste." Tom Tarpey kept his eye on Jim Kirie and enjoyed what he was seeing.

"The Blue Ribbon Committee will be holding its own press conference this afternoon at 2pm and you can ask them all the questions you like. Thank you for attending."

Tarpey quickly removed himself from behind the podium and swiftly made it through the crowd of reporters and on-lookers to his office.

"It's almost frightening that Kirie was the only one to lose his cool."

"Frightening isn't a strong enough word. You're the huge burr in their saddle, especially without them having either Enger or Novelli on that council."

"Which gives them all the more reason to ensure that I become a non-breather."
Taking a deep breath, Tom gives a serious look to his brother and says, "Jacta Alia Est."

"What in the hell does that mean?"

"The die is cast, big brother."

• CHAPTER SIXTEEN •

"Hello, Marty? You hear? Yeh, neither you nor Enger made it. Well, how in the fuck am I s'pose to know? Course I'm sure. No. Look. We packed that place with our voters. C'mon! They had to tamper with the ballots. Sure as Hell, it's bullshit. I'm gonna have the motherfucker killed is what I'm gonna do. Look, I really don't care if he IS becoming a hometown celebrity. Celebrities die every day. Nah. No shootings. Just a nice little car accident. Sure, I'll check with the big boss first. You think I'm stupid? Yeh. Yeh. Talk to you later."

"Jesus, Harry. I don't know if I could handle Tarpey being knocked off."

"Look, Jim you little piece of chicken shit in the basket, you're in this for the full ride, or you're gonna take one. Capeesh?"

On Tuesday, the new committee met for the first time and selected their officers. The new chairman, Tova Bichel was elected primarily because she had no ties to any party, was open-minded and had no loyalties. Not to mention that many on the council felt she was a weak sister and could be persuaded their way.

After her appointment, Mrs. Bichel rose to address the committee. "I find it a great honor to be elected chairperson of this new 'blue ribbon' committee, for which I thank you. As you know, it is our role to make recommendations to the Board of Trustees on the future growth of our unique urban area. In particular, the committee will focus on proposed land use of two large parcels now containing the drive-in movie theatre and a bowling alley."

Larry Cossack leaned over and whispered into the ear of Mr. Lerner, the only other staunch Steigerwaldt supporter on the committee, "I think we just fucked ourselves."

"I agree" he whispered back. "This broad set us up for this. She's obviously got her shit together and Harry's gonna scream."

"Now, while neither property is currently under development" Mrs. Bichel continued, "each parcel has been determined to be too valuable to remain as they are now. Two months ago, the Board of Trustees had proposed that this property be made into a high density, residential area. It is our first task then, to pick up where they left off, investigate this further, and eventually make a final recommendation and proposal back to the Board of Trustees.

Mr. Warchol spoke up first. "Personally, I don't want no apartments and another several thousand people moving in here. We all know that the community can't handle that kind of influx. But besides that, as a committee, we have to make sure we propose to the Trustees that the Village gets developed the way the Village wants to be developed and not developed based upon certain people lining their pockets, if you get my drift."

This time it was Lerner whispering into Cossack's ear, "Jesus, is Harry gonna be a sneeze ahead of a fit."

Where Bill's first arrest took place.

River Grove Police Force as lead by Chief Tom Tarpey.

As a celebrity himself, celebrities would seek out Chief Tarpey.

Chief O'Hallen enters the Triangle Inn.
(1957 Chicago Tribune photograph)

The Mob was real.

Elmwood Cemetery where John Bree
could often be found when not in Joliet.

Tucker's today.

Ott, Raffin, Donnie Williams, Ray Apt & a host of others.

Bill Ott takes centerstage surrounded by friends.

The unforgettable flamed squad car.

Joliet Prison

*The Thirsty Whale on the corner of River Road & Grand Avenue
(That's Gene & Jude's directly behind it.)*

Bill Ott with an attitude.

Bill Ott's infamous motor home.

The group cleans up for another wedding.

Bill Ott and the author, Jim Altfeld.

• CHAPTER SEVENTEEN •

Ok, Mr. Ott, what're your thoughts about what you've just read? You like it, or can I still not dot the I in the word shit?"

"You know, I really miss those Thanksgiving parties at Whites. As for Tarpey, I had to admire him for trying. I had no idea Apt was working with him, though. But I was thinking of someone who should be in your book."

"Who's that?"

"Johnny Bree? Obviously, you can't interview him, but he really needs to be a part of your story here. Hell, he was without a doubt the toughest, most athletic and strongest motherfucker in our eighth-grade class. Plus, he was one of the five in our eighth-grade class who were all fucking sixteen years old."

"No argument from me."

"You remember when Bob Baus was arguing with our third-grade teacher Ms. Prost over a parking space?" Bill cracks up thinking about it. "I mean here's a kid in eighth-grade arguing with a 3rd grade teacher over a fucking parking space."

"Well, in those years they held kids back. That doesn't happen anymore."

"Just be sure you put Johnny Bree in your book."

Winter comes cruel in Chicago, beginning in October and continues on into April. The Windy City received its name originally for its politicians, but that was changed over time to the knifing winds called The Hawk that whip their way down Michigan Avenue and blew from the Lake to South Wacker Drive. Winds that were known to literally lift and deposit pedestrians attempting to cross the Michigan Avenue Bridge right into the semi-frozen Chicago River. The City finally got smart and ran a rope along the bridge to give people something to hold on to while crossing. And on top of the wind there was the bitter cold resulting from that wind. Obviously, no one came to Chicago for its weather. You were there to work and eat, which is why jobs were usually plentiful and the food was damn good.

Chicago's suburbs received the same nasty winds that downtown Chicago had, but colder temperatures. They were known to go as low as minus 25 without a wind chill factor. With the wind chill factor, you didn't even want to think about it.

One who ignored Chicago's vicious weather was John Bree. A 28-year-old whose local address was the Forest Preserve and the Elmwood Cemetery that brandished a billboard aimed at passing motorists saying, "Slow Down. We Can Wait!" John's out of town address was the Joliet State Penitentiary where he spent the majority of his life since age sixteen. John's visits to White's Tavern weren't many, but they were certainly memorable.

"Shut the fuckin' door, already!!"

A cold blast of arctic type air shot through the front door.

Shivering a bit to get warm, Macatelli shut the door behind him. "Hey, don't look now, but I just saw John Bree heading this way."

"Who the fuck's that?"

"Oh, that's right. Betty's never seen John Bree before. It was always Earl who was here. Well, Ms. Corrigan, you're in for one helluvan experience."

"What the fuck is this idiot talking about?"

"Not What. Who. Or maybe It."

"Fuckin A, it's cold. I'll take a beer and shot a schnapps."

Bill Ott came over to the bar and leaned in toward Betty.

"John Bree doesn't get out much because he's either hidin out in the cemetery or woods, or he's back in Joliet.

"You're making this up just to creep me out."

"No. I grew up with him. As a matter of fact, Apt was always pissed because John was sent to St. Charles Reform School before he was." Bill pauses. "Ya know, I'll take a beer and a shot of schnapps, too."

"Here ya go, only why is this guy living in a cemetery?"

"John has a knack for finding warm dead bodies either in the woods or the cemetery. And every time he does, their neck is broken and their clothes are neatly folded next to the naked body.

"Oh, for Crissakes, you ARE creeping me out!"

Macatelli re-enters the conversation. "Betty, Bill ain't lyin. In another minute or two you can see for yourself. But how in the fuck he gotta outta the hospital beats the shit outta me."

"Hospital?!"

"Yeh. The sonofabitch got hit by a car last week doing thirty five. The lady who hit him knocked him right out of his shoes." Said Macatelli.

"Yeh, but after flying about ten feet, John got up and started looking for his shoes because he was complaining his feet were cold!" added Ott.

"No fuckin way."

"Way. The woman called for the cops and made them take him to the hospital."

"And he's about to walk into my bar?"

The front door flew open for the second time in the last ten minutes, only this time it was John Bree just standing in the doorway.

"Oh, my God!" Betty's mouth was open and her eyes were wide and laser focused on John. "It's gonna be a long fuckin night."

John staggered in wearing a pair of broken shoes the police had given him, a pile of rags for a coat, and a clear, smelly, paste-like gel all over his face, all the while clutching a 7-Up can and a rag like they were the most precious things in the world to him. Bill walked up and closed the door behind John.

John somehow still maintained an Arnold Schwarzenegger physique, but his brain was gone. His addiction to sniffing glue and other stringent solvents like Toluene, Bestene, and Naptha caused permanent damage over time. This was just additional damage that the guards and inmates inflicted upon him during his very early years in prison. By the time John was eighteen, he was already punch drunk.

"Ah, ah, ahn body ga, ga, got ah, ah, corter?" John asked as he smeared the glue soaked rag on his face.

"Ahn, Ahn body got a corter?" he yelled this time obviously getting agitated.

"Oh, fuck. I'm gonna be sick."

"Hold on, Betty. I got him," said Ott.

"No, you don't, I do." The soft, but firm voice came from the rear of the tavern and belonged to Ray Apt. Ray got up and carefully approached the ever-lethal John Bree.

"John, here's your quarter."

While attempting to focus on the quarter and hold the rag to his face, John set the 7-Up can down on the bowling game, spilling some of its contents in the process.

"Ah, Shit! C'mon guys, that stuff'll eat the fuckin varnish right off the board. Somebody PLEASE clean that mess up!" Betty yelled as she threw a wet bar rag toward the bowling machine.

Apt snatched the rag out of mid air and obliged her request.
John continued to stare at the quarter.

Finally, John's shaking hand holding the quarter slowly worked its way down to a pants pocket where he deposited it.

"Oh, God. Now what's he doing?"

John began peeling the pile of rags off that showed a moth eaten, stench ridden red sweater underneath. John then proceeded to ever so slowly and with much difficulty, remove the red sweater.

"Really, guys. What is he doing?"

John finally managed to pull the sweater off over his head and stood naked from the waist up.

"What a waste of a great human body," thought Betty.

At six feet and one hundred and eighty-five pounds, John could bench 440 pounds effortlessly. His physique was truly incredible. Even Ray Apt had to admire it. It was a chiseled, muscular body devoid of fat that would have given Arnold Schwarzenegger a run for his money. Even Apt had to admit that pound for pound, John was the most powerful person ever to set foot in White's Tavern. Scariest of all is that even in his glue sniffing state of intoxication, like a black mamba snake, John remained exceptionally dangerous.

"You remember how far he could throw a baseball in grade school?"

"Fuck. He had a helluva body even back then, plus he was athletic as all hell."

While in prison, John discovered the world of weightlifting where John sought and found some peace and solitude. In prison it was his escape from reality. Outside of prison, he turned to glue, toluene and naphtha.

"Why in the hell is he standing there flexing?"

"For beer and quarters. It's his way of panhandling."

"For Crissakes, now I've seen everything."

"All right, John!!" Some of the patrons began yelling as they tossed quarters at him having seen this exhibition before. A few began whistling and stomping but no one dared to venture too close to John.

"Here's a beer, John" Bill Ott said as he handed a cold bottle of Old Style to the massively built John Bree.

"Now put your sweater back on and sit down for a while. Just take it easy."

Bill kept an arm's length distance between himself and John. Not so much to keep himself out of harm's way as much as it was due to John's body odor.
"Pew! I don't know how the guy can stand himself."

"With that much glue up his nose, he can't smell shit."

"Didn't think about that."

With the few brain cells John had remaining, he reached for his sweater lying on the floor and succeeded to put it on himself, only backwards. He then stooped down on all fours to collect all the coins that had been tossed at him.

"What in the hell keeps that man going? He oughta be dead by now."

"We think he's bionic."

"He must be."

After searching for and successfully finding his pants pocket again, John deposited his booty adding it to the quarter Ray had given him.

"Is he done now?"

"Yes, Betty, he's done."

John, still staggering a bit, somehow remembered to grab his glue filled 7-Up can off the bowling game. But then, he also remembered he needed to urinate.

"I gah, gah, gahtta piss."

"That's it. Please get him the fuck outta here. He can flex all he wants but he ain't gonna be taking a piss in my bar!"

With that, Betty headed for the phone and began dialing the cops keeping her eyes on John the entire time who was now shuffling his way toward one of the bathrooms. Fortunately, it was occupied.

With receiver in hand, Betty pleaded with Ray, "Ray, for God's sake, don't let him do anything I'm gonna regret!"

John turned from the bathroom and slowly stumbled back towards the front door of the Tavern.

"Yeah. This is Betty over at White's. I was callin about John Bree, but it appears he's leaving. Fuck yes, he's scary! I KNOW he's dangerous. Why ya think I'm calling you guys!!??!! No, don't come over. He's heading out the door now."

Ott held the front door open. John ambled out and was gone.

"Shut that fuckin door before that thing comes walking back in here!!" Betty sat down and poured herself a shot of Jack Daniels and downed it.

"You guys grew up with him?!?!"

"Yeh. I'm telling you. He was probably the greatest athlete this town ever produced."

"What in the fuck happened to him?"

"Just to give you an example, his parents locked him out of the house when he was four or five fuckin years old because they wanted to be alone."

"No way! Nobody does that!"

"Yeh, way. So, in retaliation, John, set fire to the garage and that's really when it all started."

"Good Lord."

"He was sent to St. Charles by the time he was eight and from there he was in Joliet at sixteen."

"Sad thing is he always felt better off IN Joliet than he did being out."

"Yeah, he and Cliff Parry once held up the Clark gas station on Grand over by Webster and then sat near the pumps waiting for the cops to arrest them."

"How old was he then?"

"Nineteen."

Betty poured another shot of Jack and downed it.

Sitting quietly by himself and going unnoticed was Georgie Crider. A devious fungus who unbeknownst to pretty much everyone, had become one of John's "Lovers" over the years.

For John to have become a homosexual is quite understanding considering all the years he spent in prison. How he and Georgie Crider hooked up was anyone's guess.

"I know where that motherfucker's gonna take a piss" Crider thought to himself as he slipped out the back door unnoticed, except for the blast of cold air that came rushing in behind him.

"Who the fuck was that?"

"Beats me."

"I, I, I, I, I'll kkkk-kkkk- kill yah yah ffffffffucker!! You're Dead!!"

"Who the fuck's that?"

"It's coming from outside."

"John?"

"Sounds like John."

"Can't be John."

"Sounds like John."

"Well get the hell out there and take a look already!!"

Without donning coats, Apt, Ott and Betty went out the front door.

"Oh, shit!"

Between the Tavern and Post Office next door there was a space of less than two feet. The perfect spot for John to take a piss.

"Somebody wedged the poor asshole between the buildings!"

"I wouldn't want to be that somebody."

"How we gonna get him outta there?"

"Call the fire department."

"You kidding?"

"No. Call the fire department. They'll get him outta there."

"I'm gonna get something to throw over him or he's gonna freeze to death out here."

Georgie Crider, thinking it would be a good idea at the time, had come around the Tavern and walked out into the street so John wouldn't notice him. When in a direct line with John, Crider took a running start and checked John from behind wedging him in between the two buildings.

"I'll get a blanket. You call the fire department."

An old worn blanket was wrapped around John as cops, firemen, paramedics, lights, sirens, and spectators flooded the area. The fifteen-degree Fahrenheit temperature seemed to have little effect on the spectators.

"Wow. This is almost as exciting as when Ronnie was on top of Al's Grill."

"How in the hell did he get himself stuck in there?"

"Hell, if I know. We just heard him yelling."

"Didn't he just get hit by a car last week?"

"Yeh. And now he's back in the news again."

"Larry, how in the fuck are you guys gonna get him outta there?" Bill Ott was asking the Fire Chief.

"Oil."

"Oil??"

"Yeh. We just take some 20-weight oil and pour it over his shoulders. He'll come out slicker than shit."

The firemen cut away John's sweater while a strong thick rope was tied to John's waist. The four quarts of oil was working its way down John's broad shoulders and lubricating the two walls and filling into the crevices.

"I, I, I'm cccccc col, cold."

"I know John. You'll be out in a jiffy."

"All right, guys. Pull."

The slack on the rope was quickly taken up as the four firemen gave a firm tug on the rope. John's buttocks and legs were slightly elevated as the oil continued doing its job.

"That's it. He's coming loose."

In less than a minute, John popped free from between the two buildings, landing on his butt. No one remembered to catch him. Or more than likely, no one wanted to.

"I, I, I'm c-c-c-cah- cold."

Several blankets were piled on top of John. Betty, in spite of her tavern toughness, had been inside making hot cocoa for the Wedged Wonder.

"Here's some cocoa John. Drink it slow."

"C'mon. Let's get him inside."

"OH, NO!! I'll give him the cocoa, but I don't want this creep back in my fuckin bar ever again. Get him the fuck outta here."

The Tavern regulars returned inside as the police, firemen and paramedics dispersed. John got to spend a free, warm night in the River Grove jail. Missing though was the glue filled 7-Up can that was left sitting where John had left it. In spite of all the commotion, the can remained upright next to the very spot John had been uprooted.

"How in the hell could he get wedged in there like that."

"Simple. You wanna know a secret?"

"You ain't bright enough to have a secret!"

"No, this really is a secret."

"Ok, what's the secret?"

"Georgie Crider."

"Who?"

"Georgie Crider. Grew up over on Julian Terrace with his two brothers and a sister. He was sitting in the back. Took me a while to recognize him. Must've been him who went out the back door."

"You think he smashed John between the buildings while the guy was takin a piss?" That's crazy!"

"I think they were having a Lover's Quarrel."

"Oh, don't even go there."

"Look. John's showing off his body which pisses Crider off, so he sneaks out and checks John from behind and puts him between the two buildings."

"You mean this guy Crider and John Bree have a thing going on? Oh, fuck. Just that thought of that makes me want to puke."

Betty downs a third shot of Jack Daniels and makes a face. "Yechhh!"

Nine days later, according to the paper, *"River Grove Police pulled a body identified as Georgie Crider out of a pond in the woods near the Des Plaines River. Crider was found face down in a pond about 100 yards west of 1st Avenue and one block south of Fullerton. In addition to the body being naked from the waist down, the Medical Examiner confirmed Crider's neck had been broken, and determined that the broken neck was the cause of death and not accidental drowning as had been first thought. Apparently, Crider had been in the pond for several days."*

Apparently, too, John had gotten even.

• CHAPTER EIGHTEEN •

Christmas was actually quite festive in the Tavern with most everyone getting into the spirit of the holiday. Betty had the lights, tinsel, mistletoe and an assortment of decorations put up a couple of days after Thanksgiving. Then someone had the brainstorm to have a grab bag party.

"I think having a grab bag was a great idea."

"Guaranteed, it'll be interesting." Bill Ott said with a hint of sarcasm in his voice.

"You know, Bill. You're the reason aliens won't visit this planet."

"Thanks, Elaine. I'll keep that in mind."

Brian King outdid himself by dressing up as Santa and carried around a large postal sack he'd stolen off a mail truck. Fortunately, it was empty when he stole it.

"All right, boys and girls, put your gifts here in Santa's sack and let's get this show on the road."

'Wow, Brian. Nice to see you wearing men's clothes again."

"Cute, Elaine, now go buy me a beer…. Please."

The crowd began dumping their wrapped and unwrapped gifts in the postal sack.

"Ok, so go over to Betty at the bar there and pull ONE, as in not two or three or a handful of numbers out of the bowl and that will determine the order we grab."

"I'm duly impressed. Everyone is behaving themselves and really getting into this."

"Give 'em time, Betty. The drugs haven't kicked in, yet."

The excitement and merriment continued to build as the Christmas music poured from the juke box, grab bag gifts were being opened and the level of intoxication increased tremendously.

"AHHHHHH! NO! Fuck, NO!!! This is really fucking sick. Who did this?!?!"

It was Betty doing the screaming. She opened the grab bag gift she had just pulled out of the postal sake, only to discover the Raffin brothers' contribution... a dead cat.

Rick Raffin, realizing a diversion was in order slipped a twenty-dollar bill to Donny Williams' new girlfriend of the night and in a flash, her top came off and she was bouncing bare breasted to the beat of Frosty the Snowman being sung by none other than Gene Autry.

"You know, this place just never ceases to amaze me."

"Yeh, ain't it wonderful?"

"Hey, you should've been with us the other night when we went downtown for dinner at Benihana's."

"You did?"

"Yeh, about a dozen of us went. You know how the chef cooks right in front of you flipping knives and setting fire to the grill?

"Sure."

"Well, the highlight was when Bill tossed an entire bag of magic mushrooms on the grill while the chef was cooking up the vegetables."

"What'd he do?"

"The chef? His eyes got big, but he never stopped cooking."

"That had to be one helluva meal and a drive home."

Once everyone had gotten over the gift-wrapped dead cat, the laughter and merriment continued.

"Hey, everyone, I got an announcement to make!" It was Bill with that foghorn booming voice of his cutting through the pandemonium.

"Hey, you fucking jagoffs, shut the fuck up!"

"We're singing!"

"Mac, just because you can talk doesn't mean you should sing. Shut the fuck up for a minute."

"Who's talking?"

"I am."

"You know your father would be very disappointed if he ever saw you dressed like you are now."

"DT. It's me, Elaine. Not Bill."

"It is?!? What sign are you?"

"Caesarian."

"Oh, sorry."

"You know, DT, if your IQ ever hits 50, I'd sell."

"Hunh?"

"Never mind. Just go lay down next to Marshall Sorenson over there and you'll be fine."

"Thank you, Elaine. You're a gem."

DT was about to lay down when he cried out, "Oh, shit!"

Elaine turned quickly to see. "Now what?"

"Sorensen just pissed himself again."

"Hey. Never stand between a dog and a fire hydrant. You'll be fine, DT."

Bill, now getting more frustrated trying to quiet the crowd down yells over to Elaine, "Elaine, help me out here."

"Why? You're doing a great job!"

Betty then walked over and pulled the plug on the juke box causing the place to become almost eerily quiet. "That oughta do it."

"Thank you, Betty! I just want everyone to know that I got Elaine pregnant and we're getting married!"

"Well if that ain't worth celebrating what is" Betty spoke aloud to herself as she plugged the juke box back in.

"All right, Otto!"

"Congratulations, Elaine!"

"Thanks, Brian. Ya mind if I ask you a question?"

"Not at all."

"How'd you ever make it out of your mother's birth canal?"

"Elaine, I assure you I wasn't born this size and that your baby will be just fine."

The party continued well into the early morning, dead cat and all.

"Hey, Rick. The dead cat was a little over the top, even for this group."

"Yeh, but it sure livened up the place."

"I'll give you that!. By the way, you still working for Maytag?"

"Nah. Me and Terry went to some training school for service people in Newton, Iowa last month and wrecked the place. We got pretty wasted and Terry ended up driving a service truck through one of their fucking buildings. They fired him and put me on probation."

Bill Ott gives Rick an inquisitive look, "And?"

"And I said, fuck that, and quit."

"So, now what're you doing?"

"I started my own repair business and call it Doc Rick's Washer and Dryer Service. Got my own truck and tools, plus Terry's helping out. Outside of that, I'm working for Tarpey."

Bill was about to take a swallow from the bottle of Old Style he was holding and stopped. "Come again?"

"I'm a reserve cop."

"Holy Kerfuck! So, what the hell's with Tarpey's car?"

"I don't know. Between the car and the Lone Ranger get up, I think he's cracked."

"I heard his wife's divorcing him. Maybe that put him over the top."

"How long you expect to be a cop?"

"Till I can get Doc Rick's off the ground, or until they haul Tarpey off to Dunning."

"A mental institution most certainly could be in his future."

"So, Bill. When you going to do this great thing?"

"Get Elaine pregnant? I did that already!" Bill responds with a laugh.

"No, asshole, the wedding?"

"Sometime in January. Probably at the American Legion Hall."

"How about the honeymoon?"

"February. We figure the weather here'll be a motherfucker, so we'll go down to Miami to soak up some rays and score come toot. Sorta mix business with pleasure."

Bill's face suddenly took on a look of horror. "Oh, shit! I'm sorry, Raffin. I was just kidding, honest. I forgot you're a fucking cop, now." Bill lets out a huge laugh and Raffin laughs right with him.

> *"Oh, the white cat piddled in the black cat's eye*
> *And the black cat said 'ere bly me!'*
> *And the white cat said 'you silly sod, you*
> *Shouldn't stand behind me!"* Scottish Folksong

• CHAPTER NINETEEN •

With the holidays behind them, the "Blue Ribbon" advisory committee, headed up by Mrs. Bichel, were planning their fourth meeting since they appointed her chairperson. The prior meetings had been interesting for Mayor Tarpey and aggravating for Harry Steigerwaldt, as Steigerwaldt's plans were grinding to a halt.

"Do you fucking believe this goddamn committee?!? Fucking Warchol stands up and opposes any friggin growth in certain areas of the village; Czajka says growth is inevitable; and Piscopo agrees, but adds it should be sane growth, whatever the fuck that means! I'm telling you, Harry, it's like Tarpey wrote the script and everyone is just acting out their parts."

"What happened when you brought up the issue of re-zoning?"

"Bichel started complaining that re-zoning can bring property values down and it's like taking money out of a property owner's bank account. So, I asked that we as members of the committee do not base our recommendations on black and white comparisons about growth. That simple comparisons would be more effective."

"How'd that go over?"

"Like a fart in church! I no sooner got my words out when Tom Conrad says we should preserve and maintain our residential environment and that the lifeboat will only hold so many. I mean, Jesus H. Christ, we're getting nowhere fast."

"I think it's time to start lobbying some of these committee members. Who do you think are the easiest to win over? I know Bichel ain't one of them."

"I'd start with Warchol. That fuckin Polack would sit up, beg and rollover for a couple of grand."

"Who else?"

"In order, I'd say Warchol first, Cossack and maybe Piscopo. You already have Eggert. As you said, forget about Bichel and also forget about DeCoste and Conrad. They're staunch Tarpey people. Czajka is hard to read and obviously, I'm with you."

"Ok. I'll have Warchol approached first, then we'll just go on down the line till we have a majority."

"Call me slow, but now I gotta agree with your idea from a month or two ago. Let's just get rid of Tarpey and stick our own guy in as Mayor. Senior Councilman Jesperson is next to be Mayor if anything happened to Tarpey."

"Yeh, I know" responded Steigerwaldt smiling.

It was early so the Tavern wasn't overly crowded. Ott and Raffin were there sipping on a couple of Old Styles.

"So, Bill, you stll think Tarpey's nuts?"

"Hey. Any guy who dresses like the Lone Ranger, has a squad car with flames painted on it, carries not one, but two Smith & Wesson's on his hip like he's Wild Bill Fucking Hickock, and writes to the Olympic Committee demanding that the Olympics be held here in River Grove ain't exactly playing with a full deck. Yeh. I think he's a sandwich or two shy of a picnic."

"Yeh, but in what other town can you have a whacked-out Mayor and Police Chief all in one guy?!?" Both laugh before pounding down another Old Style.

"I didn't hear about Tarpey going after the Olympic Committee. Where'd you hear about it?"

"You didn't see his picture in the Tribune? He was also in the Daily News."

"Nah. You're kidding."

"Seriously. He made the third page of both papers. He says he's the new law and order in town. The picture was of him in his Lone Ranger Outfit standing next to his flaming squad car."

"You gotta be kidding."

"No. They quoted him about his going after the Olympic Committee demanding that the Olympics be held in River Grove."

"God. Remember when he got Ronnie off the roof of Al's Grill? He'd probably shoot him down now instead of talking him down.

"You gonna invite him to your wedding?"

"Ronnie? Of course."

"No. Tarpey."

"Oh, fuck yes! With him there we're sure to get on the ten o'clock news!"

The wedding went off as planned as the guests were all well primed and loaded before, during and after the ceremony. The bride's parents wept through the entire ordeal and not because they were losing their daughter.

"It was a real fucking mess. I mean Danny fucking puked all over himself in the damn car while driving to the church. Then he pulls over and passes out."

"Sounds swell, DT. "

"It was awful! I had to drag him out of the car, clean him up, clean the car up and put him back in the driver's seat. And man did it stink!"

"You put him back in the driver's seat?!?!"

"Yeh! You think I'm gonna sit where he just puked?"

DT and Danny Drew were just two of the over forty representatives from the Tavern to show up for the wedding. Even more than that were in attendance at the reception.

The best thing that could be said about the reception was that only four fights broke out; the band left on their own accord, and without incident; and the police were not called.

"Looks like the bride and groom are heading out for the airport."

"I'd be willing to bet that we're the only two people to see them leave."

"I'd be willing to bet no one cares that they left. This is one helluva party with or without them."

Moving to the far back of the Legion Hall, Tom Tarpey and Ray Apt continue their conversation.

"Look, Ray, I seriously think Harry Steigerwaldt has had it and is beyond pissed off. I think he's going to make his play. I know you and my brother have been talking, so what did you two come up with?"

Ray squints, lowers his voice to a whisper and barely moves his lips. "It's time. Just follow my play and don't get all pissed off with the outcome."

"What in the hell are you talking about?"

'THIS, YOU MOTHERFUCKER! You've been harassing me, trying to pin shit on me left and right and I've had it! "

Much of the crowd was now turning to see the commotion.

"Well, fuck you because I'm gonna nail you, yet."

"Either get off my case, Mr. Lone Ranger, or you're gonna wish you had."

"You know who you're talking to? I ought to run you in right now!"

"But you won't cuz you're all smoke and no substance you pansy assed piece of shit!" Their faces were only inches apart as the spit was flying.

"That's it. You're under arrest!"

"No. That ain't it, this is!!"

Apt connected a straight uppercut to Tarpey's chin knocking him woozy but not out. He'd taken just enough off the punch. Tarpey staggered and took a mandatory eight count with Apt glowering over him like Ali over Liston.

"Chew on that for a while, but just know you and me ain't through, yet." With that Ray grabbed his leather jacket and left the reception.

Bill and Elaine made it to O'Hare Airport in plenty of time thanks only to the planning by Elaine's parents. They had a cab waiting for them outside the American Legion Hall at exactly 8pm. Their plane took off on time at 9:17pm and they arrived in Miami six hours later, plus one time zone change.

"Fuckin, Ay, Elaine, I feel like homemade shit."

"Don't blame me. You're the one who had to get here to meet the boat. I'm just two months pregnant and here for our honeymoon."

As they were walking through the Miami airport and towards baggage claim, Bill hesitated. "Elaine, hold on for a second. I want to get a paper." Bill's eyes were blood shot and he looked like he'd just spent the night on a red eye. A cigarette dangled from his lip as the smoke curled up in his nose and eyes, causing him to squint a bit.

"Bill, if I stop walking now, I'm gonna need a jump start to get me going again."

"Fucking bright in here, ain't it?"

"Bill, just go buy your paper and quit talking. Neither of us could add up a couple of zeroes with a calculator right now."

Bill was carrying his coat in his right hand and used his left to grope for a quarter in his pants pocket. "Elaine, help me, for Crissakes. I can't find a goddamn quarter. Plus, I think my hand's stuck in these friggin tight jeans."

"That's it. I'm going home."

"You crazy? Home is 2000 miles away and we just got here!"

Reaching into her purse, "Here Bill. Here's a fucking quarter. Just shut up."

Bill took the quarter and deposited into the self-serve newspaper vending machine, opened the door and began screaming.

"ELAINE! ELAINE!! I'M FUCKED AND DEAD!"

Whipping herself around on a dime and now wider awake than she'd been in the past four hours, Elaine had had it. "Bill, be more positive, we just got here."

"Ok, I'm probably dead!"

"Bill, right now, if you're looking for sympathy, look it up in the fucking dictionary and you'll find it somewhere between shut up and syphilis, but you ain't gonna get it from me."

"Elaine, listen to me, we've been fucked."

"No, Bill. I've been fucked. I'm the one who's pregnant, remember?"

"Elaine, you can read my lips or read this fucking paper. Either way, we're fucked."

'FEDERAL AUTHORITIES CONFISCATE 20 TONS OF COCAINE ABOARD THE CONTAINER SHIP THAYA

According to Federal authorities, on February 12, the MSC Thaya was making its way into the Miami Harbor for a stopover at the Port of Miami when it was intercepted by boats carrying about a dozen armed US Customs, Border Protection, and other Federal agents.

Agents then climbed a rope ladder onto the container ship and checked first to see if locks on the steel containers that hold millions of dollars-worth of trade goods were intact. According to the lead Customs Agent, "The seals on some boxes didn't look right which caused us to escort the 1,031-foot-long ship to the port of Miami. The next morning, we X-rayed then opened seven of the boxes, which is when we found bales upon bales of cocaine. All told, we confiscated 39,525 pounds of cocaine, which had a street value of about $1.3 Billion, and we arrested twelve people on charges of importing nearly 20 tons of cocaine from Columbia.'

"That was our ship. That was our connection. There goes our honeymoon."

"Look dear husband of mine, at least it got busted BEFORE you got on it. Now let's get out of this airport and to our hotel. The honeymoon may be a bust for you, but it's a day at the beach for yours truly."

"I was counting on that score."

"Look. The last time the boys in blue nailed you, you had 300-one-pound bricks of weed. Imagine what they'd do to you this time. Consider yourself lucky and now let's go."

Bill was seething.

"Bill, do not rip the shit out of that paper. Just throw it in the trash and let's go."

Bill obediently threw the newspaper into the trash and followed his wife down the hall, mumbling to himself the entire time.

Back in River Grove, the local paper was carrying a different story that covered the fifth meeting of the "Blue Ribbon" advisory committee. "Last night, City Planning Commissioner, Jim Rabjohn said, 'The American Dream is a nice home and a nice job to pay for that home. Now that dream is in conflict in some areas of the village." Rabjohn went on to warn, 'There are no easy answers. It's easy to be in favor of Pro-Growth or No-Growth. My guess is that the answer lies between the two." With representatives from Wilson Sporting Goods in attendance and listening intently, he then added, 'We don't want to send out signals to major corporations that they're not welcome here, while on the other hand we don't want to tell the residents that have lived in the neighborhood their entire lives that their neighborhood is now going to be destroyed in the name of progress.'"

An analysis by the Village Staff made it clear that the area could not keep growing unchecked. They pointed out that while water and electrical systems could be greatly expanded with proper funding, their preliminary traffic studies indicate there are limits to the capacity of this area's street system regardless of the amount of money available should the growth be too overwhelming. Their recommendation was for careful planning and further investigation into possible street redesigns."

"Fuck yes, I read the paper!" Harry Steigerwaldt, Sr. was screaming into the telephone he had just answered.

"Jesus Christ, I was at the goddamn meeting! Yes, I know what happened. No, I don't know what we're going to do. What?!? I know they won't wait that long. Look. I told you we needed to get rid of Tarpey and you didn't agree with me. Bullshit! Talk to me at Tarpey's funeral and not before. Yeh, well fuck you, too."

"Who was that Harry?"

"Marty Vaccaro. I swear Tarpey's gonna get me bumped off before I get him gone. "

"You don't really think Tarpey would put out a contract on you?"

"It's gotta hurt to be that stupid you idiot. Our own people are going to kill me if this bullshit committee keeps dragging things out."

Five days later the honeymooners returned home to once again preside over their minions and reign as King and Queen of White's Tavern. They had just missed Mitchell Sorenson's funeral. He died of an overdose the night of their wedding. Elaine's parents were still crying and not about Mitchell Sorenson.

"What's this bullshit that Tarpey's gone, and everyone thinks Apt did it?"

"I don't think it's bullshit, Otto. All I can tell you is that Tarpey's gone, his squad car's gone and Apt is gone."

"This makes no sense."

"It does if you'd seen the fight they had."

"What fight?"

"Right after you and Elaine took off for the airport, Apt beat Tarpey like a three-egg omelet and told him there was more coming. We all figured this is now the more."

"Holy Shit. Ray's snapped."

• CHAPTER TWENTY •

"It's been two weeks, Ray. I gotta get back before Harry Steigerwaldt really fucks the town over."

"I agree, but not yet. Steigerwaldt's guard is down because he, like everyone else figures I did you in."

"So, let's pack and get me back to River Grove."

"No. You're staying here for another week. I'm going back to stir some shit up first."

"What are you talking about?"

"I'm going back with your car and create a few diversions, just to buy us some time and some influence. THEN you can come home."

"No way am I staying here another week."

"Look, Tom. You've trusted me and your brother this far, just go the extra mile with us. We got a plan and it's gonna work. It's worked so far, hasn't it?"

Apt and Tarpey had been hiding out in Oxford, Wisconsin for the past two weeks, staying at a small Best Western motel, under the alias' of Steigerwaldt and Kirie. The night clerk found the squad car a bit strange, but thought it was none of his business to inquire.

Ray tossed the few belongings he had into his gym bag, grabbed the keys off the nightstand and headed for the door.

"Ray, you're going to have the entire Leyden Township after you if anyone sees you with that car."

"Like I didn't know that?" Ray laughs. "Hang loose, stay loaded and I'll see you in a week."

"A week?!?"

"One week."

"What if you get arrested, or worse, someone knocks you off? Then what?!?"

"Call your brother or start hitchhiking back."

With that parting advice, Ray closed the door behind him, started up the monstrous squad car, and sped off for River Grove. He arrived, just as planned at 2:30am. He drove straight to 8645 Carey Avenue, a friend's home near the forest preserves and Des Plaines River, pulled into the driveway, and stopped in front of the old garage in back. Ray exited the vehicle, pulled up the heavy and unlocked wooden garage door, propped it open, and climbed back inside the car.

"Time to put you away for a few days." He said to the car as he drove it into the garage. He then scribbled out a note to his buddy that read, 'Mort, Don't even think about looking in your garage for the next couple of days. Thanks. RA'

Ray closed the garage door, carefully placed the folded note between the back porch door and its moulding, and slipped back into the night. But not before grabbing the red, one-gallon can of gasoline Mort kept in the garage for his lawnmower.

"I'm telling you that this stinks!"

"You're telling me?!? Either we find Tarpey and get his ass back here, or this whole planning thing is going to blow up in our face. Steigerwaldt's been working overtime since Tom disappeared."

"I'm beginning to think Harry did the deed just to make everyone think it was Ray."

"I'm torn. One, because everyone saw Apt deck Tom at the wedding. But two, I wouldn't put anything past Harry Steigerwaldt, Sr. Either way, Tom's going to show up dead or alive."

"That's what they said about Jimmy Hoffa."

"Dead or alive he better show up soon, or it ain't gonna matter one way or another. I mean look what just happened. Three weeks ago, the committee voted that all apartment developments be restricted to medium density, 58 units per acre. Last night, with Tom out of the picture, they overturned that decision and two of Steigerwaldt's proposed apartment complexes can suddenly exceed the medium density rule. Why?" Answering his own question. "Because there ain't no Tom Tarpey to stop them, especially since Senior

Councilman Jesperson is now acting mayor."

"So, who switched their votes?"

"Both Warchol and Piscopo."

"Which means Steigerwaldt's money got to both of them."

Harry Steigerwaldt, Sr. hadn't been happier since his first wife died.

"Can you believe our luck?!? Apt wastes Tarpey and we're clean as a whistle. God, I love that guy!"

"Easy, Harry" Kirie responded. "There are State, County, and local cops looking all over for both of those guys. And they can't find either of them. It's not adding up unless someone took them both out."

"Who cares as long as the pain in the ass Tarpey's gone?"

"It's just weird."

"C'mon. This is Ray Apt. He's a mechanic, not a kidnapper. He wasted him. Goodbye Tarpey, and hello, River Grove."

"But if Apt did knock off Tarpey, who gave the order?"

At that night's council meeting, vice chairman and community development director Jim Rabjohn had to break the planning commission deadlocked tie on a recommendation concerning two of Steigerwaldt's high density apartment proposals. Rabjohn's vote overturned last week's vote that all apartment developments in "sub-area two," including the two proposed high density developments be allowed to exceed the normal restriction of 58 units per acre. Rabjohn's deciding vote put the restriction back on the buildings, meaning Harry Steigerwaldt could only build 189 apartment units instead of the 243 he had hoped to build.

"That fucking, asshole! How'd we ever end up deadlocked in the first place?!?!"

"Actually, Harry. We got off pretty easy. The residents of the area were never notified of either tonight's meeting or the one we held last week. Let's just say they're more than pissed off. And imagine how pissed off they're going to be when they find out that 189 units are going in, instead of the agreed to 29 units per acre."

"Fuck them. We should've gotten the 243 units, not the 189. It still sucks as far as I'm concerned."

While Harry Steigerwaldt, Sr. was attending the joint Planning Board/Board of Trustees meeting, Ray was outside studying his own next move.

"Excuse me, is this Harry Steigerwaldt's car?" Ray asked the bodyguard slash chauffeur sitting behind the wheel of the large Lincoln Town Car.

"Fuck off!"

"What?!? I can't hear you. Put the window down." Apt yelled back as the chauffeur's large chunky finger hit the power window button bringing the window down.

"I said, Fuck Off."

The chauffeur barely got the words out before Ray unleashed a devastating fist into his victim's face. Another nose notched in Ray's belt.

The driver slumped in the seat unconscious. White bone was showing through where his nose used to be. His face splattered in blood as both eyes were turning black. Ray lit the Molotov cocktail he prepared for the occasion using the gasoline he'd taken from the garage and tossed it through the open window toward the backseat.

"Sweet dreams, asshole." Ray once again slipped into the cover of darkness as the large Lincoln sat ablaze and eventually exploded. River Grove's volunteer fire department was on the scene containing the fire. The driver was long since dead.

"Who in the hell keeps fucking with me?!?"

"I don't know, Harry, but this is too fucking nuts."

Harry Steigerwaldt and Jim Kirie just stood staring at the flames.

As he headed back towards the Tavern, Ray saw what he was looking for... a phone booth. He quickly ducked inside it, unscrewed the light bulb and dropped a dime into the slot.

"White's!" Betty answered.

"Yeh. Is Otto there? Yeh, Otto!!"

"This is Otto, who the fuck's this?"

"Ott you asshole, it's Apt!"

"Raymond, you dumb fuck, why'd you ruin my wedding by beating up Tarpey and then kidnap the sonofabitch? I hope the hell you didn't kill him!"

"Bill, just shut up and listen. Tarpey's alive and well and that's all I can tell you for your ears only. What I need from you are some ludes."

"Ray, you're fucked. You have every cop in the state looking for you and you call me for quaaludes?"

Quaaludes, also known as Disco Biscuits, Wagon Wheels, or 714's, are a synthetic barbitual-like drug that acts as a sedative, depressant and hypnotic lasting anywhere from five to eight hours. Once in your system it slows your speech, causes deep muscle relaxation, uncontrollable body movement and messes with your thinking. Usually kicking in thirty minutes after taking them, the person "Luding Out" cannot think clearly enough to make any kind of an informed decision, pretty much loses touch with reality, and would fall asleep and then come to, completely uncertain of their surroundings and themselves.

"Yeh. They're not for me. They're for a friend, but I gotta have them."

"Ok, pal. All I got are the 300-milligram. How many, where and when?"

"A dozen. Just wrap them in tin foil and shove them up the drainpipe on the side of the wall at White's."

"You in town?"

"Not yet, but soon."

"How soon?"

"Soon enough. Just do it."

"You owe me, asshole."

"I'll pay you back only if I don't get killed first."

"Just don't lose your teeth, Ray. You look ridiculous without them."

"I'll keep that in mind, Bill. Thanks. Later."

"Later."

"What a fucking maniac."

"Who were you talking to?"

"A wrong number. I gotta go."

Bill left the Tavern and headed home to grab the quaaludes. On his way, he drove by the remains of Steigerwaldt's Lincoln Town Car.

"Hey, Ryndak! Pat!!" Bill bellowed from his car at the police officer.
"What the fuck's this?"

"Somebody took offense to Harry Steigerwaldt's car and limo driver."

"I guess! Thanks, Pat!"

Bill hit the gas and sped off down Grand Avenue headed for home. Speaking to no one but himself, "Fucking Apt. He's already here."

Apt quickly left the phone booth and headed for Steigerwaldt's Realty.

"Harry, who in the hell do you think is doing this to you? It could have been YOU in that car."

"Whoever it is, they're deader than last Tuesday."

"Ok, Mr. Steigerwaldt. We've filed all the reports and thank you again for answering all of our questions. There will be a continuing investigation into this matter and rest assured we will do all we can to catch the sonofabitch."

"Thanks, officer. Much appreciated. I have complete faith and confidence that you will. Rico, my driver was a damn good guy and he's gonna be missed."

"We'll do our best to find his murderer, sir. Good night."

"Goodnight, Officer."

Steigerwaldt and Kirie walked away from the scene.

"You really believe the cops are gonna find the guy?"

"Fuck, no!! They couldn't find an elephant if it was crossing Thatcher and Grand!"

"We're you and Rico close?"

"You're kidding, right? You know damn well he only started driving for me two days ago. Marty sent him to me and now Marty is gonna be really pissed."

Bill Ott drove back to White's, parked his car and headed for the backdoor entrance. Clumsily, playing with his keys as he walked to the door, he allowed the keys to fall from his hand and land near the drainpipe. In one swift motion, the keys were retrieved and a dozen ludes wrapped in tinfoil had been stuffed up the drainpipe.

"Otto, where'd you go?"

"Let's see. Gee. I forgot already."

"You hear about Harry Steigerwaldt's car and driver?"

"No. What happened?"

"Somebody wasted Harry's driver and set the car on fire. Kaboom!"

"Sounds more like something Harry Steigerwaldt would have had done than something someone would have done to him."

"I'm not following that?"

"What a surprise."

"Oh, I get it. You still think Harry Steigerwaldt is tied to the mob."

"And you still believe in the Easter Bunny, Santa Claus and the Tooth Fairy. Get me an Old Style, Betty and drop it."

The 2AM closing time had arrived. "Ok, you derelicts, everybody out. You're all done and I'm going home."

Betty succeeded in getting the last patron to leave at 2:24am. By 2:47am she had the place relatively squared away for the early morning re-opening. The cash was counted and the booze all locked up. "It might not be the classiest joint, but it's mine!" she thought to herself as she exited out the back door after having locked the front door from the inside. Now standing on the stoop outside she grabbed the doorknob with both hands prepared to slam the big heavy solid core door shut. The keys were already in the lock and all the money was inside her purse which was tucked under her left armpit. Placing his right hand firmly over her mouth from behind, Ray Apt wrapped his left arm around her waist and lifted her up. In one deft move, he'd kicked the door open wider and deposited Betty, gently back inside the Tavern, kicking the door shut behind him.

"Betty, whatever you do, do NOT start screaming when I take my hand off your face. It's me, Ray."

Back inside the friendly confines of White's Tavern, Betty appeared rather composed as she turned towards him. Ray quickly ducked as first the purse came flying at him, followed by a bar stool, a beer can and a bar rag.

"You fucking asshole!! What right do you have to scare the shit outta me like that?!?! I oughta call the fuckin cops and tell them where you are since the whole fucking town's looking for you! Don't you EVER do that to me again!!" Tears were streaming down her face as the mascara she was wearing began streaming along with them.

Ray just stood there smiling.

"What's so fucking funny?"

"You look like a raccoon." With that remark, she found another bar rag to throw at him.

"Jesus H. Christ, I need a drink."

All the fear, adrenaline and energy had drained out of her as Betty sat limp on the nearest barstool.

"Betty, I'm sorry, but I couldn't exactly call to let you know I was coming over here."

"You got any idea how many people are looking for you?"

"Sure. Why in the hell do you think I gotta sneak up on people like I just did you?"

"You really kill Tarpey?"

"Fuck, no. Just borrowed him for a while."

"You leave him at a pawnshop, or something?"

"How about I just say, or something? I assure you he's fine. Now, about that drink. I think we both can use one."

Betty wearily made it off the barstool and walked slowly to behind the bar. "I gotta unlock the liquor. A shot of Jack sounds good to me. How about you?"

"I'll have the same."

"So, now what?"

"Now, I'm kind of at your mercy. I need a place to sleep for a couple of hours."

"You know Fred opens at 5am for the railroad guys."

"All I need is a couple of hours."

"Well, you better sleep quick because it's already going on three. Maybe you should just crash at my place. Might be a whole lot easier and safer."

"Betty, I really appreciate the offer but you can't be involved harboring a wanted criminal. The last thing I want to do is implicate you in this. If I stay here, and anyone finds me, I just say I broke in."

They both down their shots. "Ray, I'm going home. You can stay here or at my place. I really don't care. But I've had it. Between working here all night and then getting mugged by you, I just want to go to bed and go to sleep."

"I'll stay here and will be gone before Fred gets here.. You mind if I use the cot you keep in the back?"

"Help yourself."

Betty closed the door behind her. Ray slept soundly on the cot with the dozen quaaludes still wrapped in tinfoil in his pants pocket.

"For god's sake, Harry, would you go to sleep already?!? You've been up pacing all night and it's now 3:30 in the morning!"

"How can you expect me to sleep when you know damn well someone blew up my car and killed my driver? YOU go back to bed."

"No. I can't sleep knowing you're out here walking around the house in the dark in your pajamas. C'mon back to bed and I'll give you a nice back rub."

"I don't need no goddamn back rub, I just need to think. Don"t you realize that whoever is fucking with me is just leaving me messages. If he wanted me killed, I'd be dead already."

"What guys?"

"That's what's eating at me. I think it's my own guys letting me know they've had enough."

"Why would they kill the driver if it was them?"

"Why not. It sure as hell sent a pretty strong message didn't it? Like Fuck You, strong letter to follow."

"Look, Harry. I'll call my brother Marty tomorrow and get this whole thing straightened out."

"Like hell you will. Don't call anybody. You understand me. Nobody, especially your brother. I gotta deal with this on my own."

"Shit! Hope I'm not too late." Ray mumbled to himself as the clock in his head set of his internal alarm. Squinting, he peered at the small, illuminated Sunbeam electric clock he'd plugged in next to the cot less than a couple of hours ago.

"Jesus. 4:38am. Better get out of here before Fred shows up." Ray uncoiled his large frame, sat upright and rubbed his hands over his face.

"Damn, I was tired." A quick visit to the john and Ray vanished out the back door.

"Wait till Fred tells Betty she forgot to lock the backdoor." He thought to himself knowing full well that would just rekindle her anger.

"Pretty funny."

Ray crossed Grand Avenue and headed for Steigerwaldt Realty where he broke the small pane of glass next to the back door allowing him to reach in and turn the bolt.

"Liquor cabinet's gotta be in his private office," Ray thought to himself. "There it is! Perfect!!"

Harry hadn't even bothered to lock the cabinet after he and Kirie had shared a Chivas Regal the day before. Ray unscrewed the cap from a bottle of Chivas that was still half full and dropped six quaaludes in. He next opened a new bottle of Chivas and poured a quarter of it into the bottle he had just placed the six quaaludes, then dropped the remaining six into the new bottle. He then shook both bottles.

"Whichever bottle they drink from, they're fucked."

After wiping the bottles down and removing his fingerprints from everything and anything he touched, he walked by a row of filing cabinets. "Bet there's plenty of stuff in there to put him away. But, since we both work for the same firm, I gotta take a pass." Glancing at his wristwatch, Ray realized he needed to get out of there now and leg it back to the car before the sun was completely up. Apt slept the rest of the day tucked away in the backseat of Tarpey's flame engulfed squad car.

"I can't believe that Jesperson is calling for another special council meeting because of last night's car burning. It's as obvious as the balls on a tall dog that he's on Steigerwaldt's payroll."

"Look, David. As long as Tom's not here, and it sure as hell is looking like he ain't coming back, you and me can't wait any longer to do something."

"Like what?"

"We need to tie Steigerwaldt in with the mob and expose his plans to exploit the whole damn village."

"Good luck with that. First off, even the FBI can't tie Tony Accardo to organized crime. Two, half the people in this town are just plain apathetic and don't give a rat's ass. And, the other half are just plain scared. "

"C'mon. Steigerwaldt ain't as tough as he thinks he is."

"Yeh. And neither are we!"

"So, who do you think it was that killed his driver and set fire to his car last night?"

"More than likely his own people. I don't think anyone living in River Grove would have the balls or expertise to pull that off."

"Anything back from the autopsy on the chauffeur, yet?"

David Jessen picks up the report. "Yeh. The M.E. said he was so fried there wasn't much to tell. Based on the condition of his lungs, his last breath was nothing but fire. The only odd thing the M.E. mentioned was that she thought his nose was broken." David then puts down the report and looks at Bob Tarpey.

"Bob, you look like you just saw a ghost."

"Would you repeat that."

"You look like…"

"No. Before that!"

"She thought his nose had been broken."

"That's what I thought you said."

• CHAPTER TWENTY-ONE •

"Hello, Kirie, it's Harry. Meet me at my office in twenty minutes. Yes, my real estate office. No, I really don't care how many people are in your restaurant right now. Just get your ass over to my office." Steigerwaldt hung up the phone and prepared to head out for his office.

"Harry, where you going?"

"To my office, why?"

"Because I'm worried about you."

"You didn't call your brother, did you?"

"No, you told me not to. But I think it wouldn't hurt if you did."

"Not yet. Maybe soon."

"In the meantime, Harry, I want you to carry this." Harry's wife of 26 years was handing her husband a fully loaded, nickel plated .357 magnum handgun. Now at age 57, overweight and looking old for her age, she felt a motherly sense of protection for her husband.

"C'mon, Theresa, that ain't exactly something I can carry in my pocket." Showing genuine affection, he gives her a hug. "Honestly, I appreciate the concern, but I'm already carrying a little smaller piece than that that doesn't show so much" as he pulls a small Derringer out of his pocket.

"Harry, I just don't want you dead."

"Me neither. I'm taking precautions now more than ever to cover my ass. I'll be back tonight after Jesperson's surprise meeting. Right now, I'm going to meet Jim Kirie over at my office."

The couple affectionately hugged and kissed one another goodbye.

Both Harry and Jim Kirie pulled into the parking lot about the same time.

In his eagerness, Harry unlocked and opened the back door not noticing the small broken windowpane Ray had broken a few hours before.

"I don't know about you, but I need a drink."

"It's a little early, but what the hell."

"What's your pleasure?"

"Scotch, if it ain't too smokey."

"Wow, Jim. I never realized you even had a sense of humor before. Pretty funny. Okay, two Chivas Regal's coming up."

Pouring with a heavy hand, Harry handed Jim Kirie a glass with about four fingers worth of Chivas and a couple of ice cubes.

"To your health, my good man!" They actually clanked glasses and emptied most of the contents down their throats.

"So, what are we doing here, Harry, and what was so important that I had to leave a restaurant full of paying clientele?"

"We're cleaning house. I figure either my own people are leaving me messages, or there really are a bunch of outraged citizens wanting me gone. Either way, I want to get all my files out of here."

"You bring boxes for all this crap." Kirie said eyeing the same rows of filing cabinets Ray had seen earlier.

"No, we're only taking the important files and there ain't that many." Harry answered as he set his drink down and kneeled on the floor.

"Harry, what in the hell are you doing?"

"I'm sure as hell not praying, you jerk. The door to the safe is under the rug. And while you're thinking about that, make yourself useful and pour us both another drink."

Harry pulled up on a middle section of the gold shag carpeting, as Kirie turned hearing a ripping sound.

"What's that?"

"Velcro. It's great stuff!" Harry answered as he held up a two square foot section of carpet in his hand. "We got these male and female strips of this plastic stuff they call Velcro. I just glued the female strip to the underside of the carpet and the male side to the floor. Being a shag carpet, no one could ever detect that there's a removable piece anywhere. Best toupee in town!"

"Nice, neat and clean. Think I'll have that installed in my place."

"And notice how the safe is perfectly even with the floor."

"That's beautiful! Who came up with that?"

"I did! Now where's that drink?"

Harry sat on the floor sipping his Chivas Regal with one hand, while working the combination to the safe with the other. Jim Kirie sat back in Harry's very comfortable, leather office chair and took a sizeable swig of Chivas while watching Harry.

"Harry, really. What did you need me here for?"

"Company, Jim. Just company. Plus, if anything were ever to happen to me, I want someone to know where all this stuff is."

"You're not going to give me all this stuff to hold, are you?"

"You know, Jim. Sometimes your brilliance amazes me. Of course, I'm going to give you this stuff to hold. Who else can I trust with it??"

Harry opened the door to the safe and removed several files from it.

Holding the files up for Kirie to see, "This, Jim, is the Holy Grail. It's the master plan for the Village of River Grove. This file alone contains enough evidence to get both me and you into a whole lot of trouble and maybe even a conviction."

"Then why not burn it and be done with it?"

"Because it's the master plan. It's not exactly something you can put to memory not to mention the fact that there are also a lot of plot drawings in here, too."

"You create that by yourself?"

"No, far from it. A lot of thought and planning went into this by a lot of intelligent and farsighted people. "

Suddenly and without warning, the quaaludes kicked in. Neither Harry nor Jim had any idea what was happening to them and most assuredly neither of them ever made it to the planning meeting that Jesperson had called for that night.

"All right, Ladies and Gentlemen, let's bring this Council meeting to order. Any new business?"

"Where's Harry Steigerwaldt?"

"Obviously, he ain't here."

"Anyone seen him?"

"No. And Kirie's gone, too."

"Jesus. You think..."

"Don't go there."

"What in the hell is going on around here?"

"I don't know, but I just heard a 911 call came in from Harry Steigerwaldt's office."

• CHAPTER TWENTY-TWO •

As the fates would have it, Harry Steigerwaldt, Sr. was able to eventually grab the telephone and dial 911. The volunteer fire department along with the paramedics raced to the scene. Getting there just moments ahead of them was Officer Rick Raffin.

"Jesus, are you guys fucked up, or what?!?"

"Help us. Help!"

"The paramedics will be here any minute." Eyeing the open safe and the files that still laid on the floor, Rick Raffin undid his shirt, grabbed the files and stuffed them in there. Fortunately, both Steigerwaldt and Kirie were still too far gone to have noticed.

"You'll be ok. The paramedics are here now." Raffin opened the door for the rescue squad to come in, said hello and left.

"I sure as hell hope I hear from Ray, soon."

• CHAPTER TWENTY-THREE •

The end of winter in Chicago is most welcomed as that incredible smell of spring in the air seems to awaken all and inject life back into dormant bodies. Small traces of snow still remained, but were completely ignored. It was spring with kids flying kites, riding bicycles, dogs running on wet grass and heavy winter coats replaced by light jackets. Spring is always a time for celebration, and no one did that any better than the patrons of White's Tavern.

"Just warning everyone that I saw BeeBee the ex-roller derby star skating this way in his underwear and man, is he loaded."

"Oh, No! Don't let that sonofabitch in here!"

"Shit! Too, late!!"

"Hey, Beebee! Come inside and I'll buy ya a cocktail." Apt held the door open for him as The 'Beeb' leapt through the doorway and made a perfect pirouette upon landing.

"Sumnabitch still's got it. Never even stumbled once."

"Hey Beeb, you know the difference between ignorance and apathy?

"Don't know and Don't give a shit. Where's my damn drink?"

"So, Mr. Ott, I understand you had a little excitement at your apartment last night."

"Yeh. Last night, two nights before that and five nights before that. It's my friggin landlady. Last night she calls the cops because she says we're playing the stereo too loud."

"Yeh, so?"

"So, we weren't even fuckin awake!! We were sound asleep!!! Suddenly there's a knock on the door, the guys says 'POLICE!' and I'm about to have a fuckin heart attack. Elaine runs to the bathroom and flushes down about a grand worth of dope. I open the fuckin door and the jagoff tells me he got a complaint about a loud stereo."

"I'd say she wants you outta there somethin' fierce. "

"Yeh, no kidding."

"Oh, Shit! Look out, here comes Beebee!!"

"Somebody deck that sonofabitch and throw him the fuck outta here. He's a nuisance for god's sake."

"Ah, leave him be. He ain't botherin..... HEY!!."
Macatelli barely gets the words out when Beebee body checks him into the bar.

"Beebee, goddamn it! Get your ass over here cuz I'm gonna fucking kill you!!"

Beebee skates by, gracefully lifting and absconding with a full rum and coke off the bar as he goes and exits, on skates, out the back door.

"Oh, shit, here he comes again through the front door! "

"Would somebody please deck that fucker and get him the hell outta here once and for all!!"

"Don't interrupt me, I said to the Judge, let me finish my sentence." And with that, Beebee skates out of the bar.

"Jesus Christ, that man's crazy!"

"Hey, I want everyone to know that starting today, I'm changing the hours."

"Betty, you can't just change the hours. It's in your license for god's sake!"

"Hey, I'm only reducing the number of hours we're open."

"That's bullshit. The routine's always been we drink here til 2am and then go to Rubino's. Fuckin' A, we don't even get started until 10pm!!"

"Bill, who gives a shit!?! And, what the fuck difference does it make? So, we hit the Deerhead or the Grand Tap."

"It's just stupid!"

"Say, would you assholes shut the fuck up, I'm trying to sleep over here!"

Agitated, Bill turns his attention to Kunkel. "Hey, Dickhead. Who the fuck cares about you sleeping?"

"I don't like your attitude, Bill."

"Well stand in line jagoff. You ain't the first person to tell me that."

"Just let me sleep, for Crissakes."

"Eat shit and die, jagoff. Ten million flies can't be wrong!"

Kunkel, in an obvious drug and alcohol related haze and stupor, rises from his stool in the corner and comes at Bill Ott.

"Don't tell me to eat shit, you prick! What I ever do to you?"

Ray Apt is situated between the two men.

"What the hell is it with him?", Bill asks Ray Apt, as Ray shrugs his shoulders.

"This ain't like him. He must be on speed plus the booze."

"If he is, you probably sold it to him."

"Hey, it's what I do."

Suddenly and without warning, Kunkel lunges past Ray Apt to get to Bill. Bill's arm is already cocked prepared to land a punch to Kunkel's head. Unfortunately for Kunkel, Ray reacted faster than Bill and breaks Kunkel's nose.

"Somebody better get a towel!"

"What in the hell is goin on over .... oh, shit. Get him outta here before I get sick."

Kunkel was unconscious before he hit the floor. His body was slightly twisted at the waist with an expression of pain on his blood smeared face. Warm red blood was flowing freely as a gleam of white bone showed through. Davey Joe is the first to administer first aid. Ray, almost serpent like, moves to the other side of the bar to finish his drink.

"Better get him over to Gottleib to stop the bleeding and re-set the nose."

Davey Joe is bent over Kunkel, applying pressure to his nose with a cold, wet towel.

"Somebody get me some ice."

"C'mon, I'll give ya a hand and let's just get him over to Gottleib Memorial. I'll take him in my car."

Kunkel is dragged out of the bar and loaded into Davey Joe's car. Minutes later he is on his way to the hospital.

• CHAPTER TWENTY-FOUR •

"So, Ray, before we get into your last brush with the law that put you away pretty much until now because it's only recently that you've been released, would you put an end to that final chapter with Harry Steigerwaldt, Sr., Tarpey and the Village of River Grove?"

"Sure. I met up with Raffin and I had him escort me in his squad car up to Oxford, while I was driving Tarpey's squad car. The State Troopers blockaded us on the way up, but we told them that they were better off following us than holding us if they ever wanted to see Tarpey again."

"They went for it?"

"Not at first, but eventually. They detained us right on the road for about an hour then agreed to follow us. We stopped a couple of times to pick up some beer, but eventually lead them right to Tarpey."

"Really? You stopped for Beer?"

"Yeh. What're the cops gonna do about it? Arrest us?"

"Ok, so you bring them to Tarpey."

"Yeh. He then explains the whole kidnapping thing was a hoax just to get him out of River Grove."

"You ever get nailed for Harry Steigerwaldt's chauffeur."

"No."

"What happened when Tom got back to the Village?"

"He handed the files Raffin grabbed from Steigerwaldt's office to David Jessen, who gave the whole story to the press. Raffin quit the force and made a go of it with Doc Rick's."

"And, Harry Steigerwaldt, Sr."

"Turns out he never cleared anything with Mr. DiFronzo which was a big mistake. Let's just say Harry got demoted."

"Better demoted than dead or permanently disappeared. Ok, now tell me what you did that put you away for so long."

"Well, since they can't try you or hang you for the same crime twice, I'll tell you. They, whoever THEY are, wanted someone hit and I was asked to do it. No big deal to me. I ain't got a conscience anyway."

"Can you explain how it went down?"

"Yeh. Over time, I became a good friend of his, and he trusted me. One night, I told him to meet me out in the Forest Preserves which wasn't unusual. I told him what time and where I'd meet him because I had to be somewhere before I met him and somewhere after. That meant two cars. After a couple of hours talking and taking some hits off the bottle, I tell him I gotta go. So, as we're leaving, he's a little wobbly and pours himself into his car. Once he does that, I put a couple of rounds in the back of his head. I was maybe a foot or two away from him."

"What gun?"

"A .038 automatic."

"Did you confirm he was dead?"

"You're kidding, right? Two rounds in the back of the head at close range with a .038, what would you think?"

"He's dead. What did you do then?"

"I got into my own car and drove back to White's."

"Who was he?"

"Bob Tarpey, Tom Tarpey's older brother."

"How long before they arrested you?"

"A couple of weeks. Then the trial and then back to Joliet."

"Did Tom ever suspect you?"

"No. Why would he?"

"Who gave the order?"

"You figure it out."

"How'd Tom take it?"

"I really liked Tom, but I don't think he ever really understood what working for the Outfit meant or how they work. I also don't think Tom considered the consequences of his actions."

"Explain."

"Look. Tom Tarpey just knew he was up to fighting the battle for River Grove taking on Harry Steigerwaldt. Only, he was too short sighted. He only considered he could lose his life in the fight, and that everyone else would be ok. That just never happens. Things don't happen in a vacuum and there's always collateral damage."

"So, he won the battle but at a great loss. You have to wonder if it was worth it."

"You'd have to ask him."

"But both he and his brother came to trust you."

"You ever hear that story about the scorpion asking the frog for a ride?"

"Yeh, and the scorpion promises not to sting the frog then stings him anyway?"

"Yeh. That one. Well, I'm a scorpion."

Takes a sip from his drink, "I'm sorry it was Bob because I really liked the guy, but better Bob than Tom, or me."

"Did you even hesitate for a second?"

"No, not really. Look, when you're given an order you follow it. In the Marines, if you don't follow an order, you may get shot. In the mob, if you don't follow an order, you WILL get shot. It was either Bob, or me. And eventually, someone else would have whacked Bob anyway."

"Why Bob?"

"Tom became too well known and Bob's publicity stunts worked. Tom made national news, especially with his blowing the lid off their plans to take back River Grove. It's just tough to whack a celebrity without some major repercussions. So, Bob got it."

"But, why?"

"To send Tom a message. You're only allowed to go so far and then you're not. Tom went about as far as the Outfit was willing to put up with. Even though Steigerwaldt did all this on his own, he was still representing the Outfit. And if you fuck with the Outfit, someone's gonna be toast."

"Yikes."

"I think the only thing that kept Tom from getting whacked was that Harry Steigerwaldt did it all on his own. Had the Outfit been behind it, it woulda gotten very ugly."

"You know what became of Tom?"

"Yeh. He resigned as Mayor and Police Chief, packed up his wife and the two of them moved to I think Seattle, Washington."

"What you think would have happened if Raffin hadn't grabbed those files?"

"Tarpey would have lost, Steigerwaldt would have won, and the mob would be back in River Grove."

"So, there were no victors since both Tarpey's lost, especially Bob."

"Hold it right there." Ray suddenly became deadly serious, which I have to admit scared me none too little and then some.

"You want to know something I learned in Joliet?"

"What's that?" I confess it took everything I had not to have my voice crack.

"In addition to a last meal, the guys on death row get a pair of rubber underpants for when they crap all over themselves before being electrocuted. Bob didn't need one. He never saw it coming. Personally, I'd prefer it that way."

"Interesting perspective, Ray."

"Look asshole, you're writing this stupid, fucking novel about White's Tavern, only you need to take a closer look at the people you're writing about. Death is all around them. It's a disease. And whether they drink it, shoot it, snort it, eat it, swallow it, breathe it or fuck it, everyone in that place, including you and me, are pregnant with it. Everyone in White's spends all the money they got just to get a taste of it and feel it inside their bodies. It's a taste of the grave and they get off on it. We all know death is coming, including everyone in White's, only everyone in White's just teases it until it finally comes. Bob Tarpey was no different than the rest of us. He knew death was coming, but just never knew when. And maybe he didn't tease it as much as the rest of us do, but he knew damn well that it comes nonetheless."

Ray gave a reflective thought, turned and looked at me with a look that shook me a whole lot more than somewhat and said, "Ya know what? It's ALWAYS later than you think."

Ray takes a big swallow and finishes off his drink. Looks at the bartender and asks for another. I joined him and had another one, myself.

Ray looks directly at me again, reminding me of his days staring down cobras at Brookfield Zoo. I now knew how the cobras must have felt.

"Think about this. On June 19, 1975, members of the Senate Select Committee on Intelligence arrived in Chicago to take Sam Giancana back to Washington, D.C. where he was to testify on his involvement to kill Castro. Not only was his testimony a threat to the mob, but it was also a major threat to the United States government. So, what do you think happened on that very same day?"

"You tell me."

"While Mr. Sam was making sausage and peppers in his basement kitchen in Oak Park, someone shot him in the head, then in the mouth, and put another five rounds under his chin. And whoever it was that killed him, left the sausage and peppers sizzling on the fucking range."

"Your point."

"Even when you're the top guy, it's always later than you think. And you know what else?"

"What?"

"The question still remains. Was it the mob or the CIA who killed him? Not only will no one ever know, but what difference does it make to Sam Giancana? He's still deader than last Thursday."

"Anything else you'd like to add?"

"Yeh, asshole. This. Jackie Cerone, who was one of my idols, later became acting boss in the early 1980s but was nailed for skimming money from the Vegas Casinos. He got twenty-eight-and-a-half-years on that conviction and died several days after he was finally released on parole on July 26, 1996. He never saw the conviction coming and sure as hell never thought he'd be dead just days after getting out."

"Holy shit, Ray. How you can instantly recall those dates and facts is impressive."

"I got a mind like a steel trap."

"Me, too. Only with mine, nothing gets in."

The humor obviously helped ease the tension a bit, putting a smile on Ray's face.

I decided then to focus my attention on Ray, Junior.

"Did you ever visit your dad while he was in prison?"

"Yeh. I'd go visit my dad one weekend a month in Joliet. The friggin' visiting room was surreal. Full of all kinds of people. Black, White, Yellow, Mexican, Puerto Rican. Kids, guys my age, old guys, young girls, young women, old women. No one looked happy, except for the little kids who didn't know better. We were all there for the same reason. To see someone we knew who was locked up. And the smells! All kinds of smells. PWEW!", Ray, Jr. squished his nose thinking about the smells.

"Between the body odor, food smells, diaper shit, you name it you just wanted to puke. And there was every kind of emotion going on. People crying, people yelling, people just sitting in silence with their head in their hands. The toughest part was always the end... leaving. Each prisoner could walk with their family up to the yellow line on the floor. You couldn't cross that yellow line. You just had to stand there and watch your dad walk back to his cell. Like when those guards put him back in the van and hauled him back to prison. It's just a tough thing to deal with and it happens every fuckin' time you go to see anyone in prison."

"What do you mean when the guards put him back in the van? What van?"

"When I was 13 years old, my dad somehow got out on furlough to watch me play football. I was the quarterback."

"I gotta butt in here" Ray says with pure excitement in his face. "I'm watching him play and the kid is making some incredible passes playing quarterback. Then, he stays on the field and plays defense. Next thing I know, he's got the fuckin football and he's making a run through this pack of guys, looks like Gayle Sayers and goes about 70 fuckin yards for a touchdown. I'm telling you, the kid had more moves than Allied Van Lines. Then I think, what the fuck, is he the only kid on the team cuz he's never off the fuckin field!?! "

"Wait a minute! Hold on!! Uno Momento!!! You're convicted of murder and got life, but they let you out on a furlong to watch your kid play football?? Really!?!?!?"

"Hey, good behavior and some help from my friends," Ray says with a big smile.

Turning back to Ray, Jr., "I'm sorry for interrupting the story."

"I was a good-sized kid, even at age 13. Actually, I was built pretty much like he was," Pointing to his dad.

"It really was the first time I ever had a parent in the stands watching me and I was having a really great game. Actually, it was so fuckin great that the other team's coach yells out, 'Break 33's legs!' I'm thinking, fuckin A, I'm 33!! I look across the field and I guess my dad also heard the coach yell to break my legs. Next thing I know, my dad's out of the stands in this guy's face, and it ain't pretty."

"Ray?"

"I was pissed. I tell the fuck, you take my kid's legs out and I'll take your fuckin head off one piece at a time, motherfucker. I'll punch the shit outta you. And just to make sure he understood me, I told the prick we were gonna talk more after the fuckin game."

"So, the games over, we won big, everyone's pretty much gone home, and I say, c'mon Dad, let's go. He says, 'Shut up. Just shut up.' The coach who wanted to break my legs finally shows up and looks like he's gonna cry or something. He says to my dad, 'Oh Mr. Apt, I'm really sorry, I lost control and got outta hand. I apologize for my actions. I didn't realize it was you'…. And the guy has pretty much pissed in his pants by now. Next thing I know, two guards grab my dad, load him into a van and haul his ass back to prison. I just watched as they drove off. I was like Fuck! That was my day with my dad. "

"Hey, you make choices in life. Right or Wrong. I made mine. You make yours. Only, I OWN mine. Period. And most of mine were wrong, but they were mine and I own 'em. No excuses. "

Takes another sip of his rum n' coke.

"I did my time for the decisions I made. If you want to enjoy the benefits, you also have to face up to the consequences. Not enough people do that anymore."

"Spoken like a true Existentialist."

"Well, fuck you, too!"

"I meant it as a compliment."

With that Ray smiles, gives me an endearing smack on my head and says, "Do you even know anything about Existentialism?"

"Yes, some, but I'll let you tell me."

It existed long before World War two, but really kicked in after the war because it seemed to be the answer for totalitarianism and mass society. What some people call the tyranny of the masses. What began in World War One, where individualism was on the way out with everyone wearing the same uniform and everyone looking like everyone else, Existentialism placed the highest value on individual choice and put the onus on the individual to determine his or her purpose. You ever read Samuel Beckett's play, Waiting for Godot?"

"Can't say that I have."

It's about these two guys waiting for this guy Godot to show up over a two-day period. Long story short, Godot never shows up and never will show up. And the point of the book, jagoff, because I know damn well you're gonna ask me, is that in life, nothing is ever coming with the answer or the solution and it ain't never coming. It's up to each of us as individuals to provide the answers and make the decisions. That it always comes down to, you are responsible for you."

"Well, that explains a lot of your thinking."

"Without a doubt, Nietzsche's work is the best, but right now, speaking of you are responsible for you, we need to get back to this fuckin idiot." Giving a hard glance at his son.

"Go ahead, moron. Tell him all about what an idiot you were."

"Turns out, thanks to his genes," pointing to his dad, "between the age of 13 and 16, I began filling out. I went from 5'6" to 5'11" and from 125 pounds to 162 pounds, all rock-solid muscle. For a sixteen year old kid I was pretty menacing."

"Gee. Gotta wonder where the menacing part came from."

"No surprise there, hunh?!?"

"Anyway, I guess I had some anger issues when I was about 15 or 16. I'm at Al's Grill in River Grove with my friends getting a burger and this guy out of nowhere asks me if I gotta light. I don't know why, but I reach into my pocket like I'm gonna pull outta lighter and instead pull out my fist and cold cock the motherfucker right there. He went down, like BOOM! Another time, I'm in the fuckin pool hall and some asshole bumps my stick. I broke the fuckin thing in two over his head and then beat him with the short end I was still holding."

"Is this Ray, Jr. or Bill Ott?"

"Another time, we snuck into White's and this guy is just reaching for his keys and I laid him out. I actually felt so bad about that one that I helped the guy up, bought him a drink and just left. But by then, word got back to my dad."

"So, here I am in Joliet and I'm getting calls from friends telling me my kid's out of control and way out of line. So, I called him up from Joliet and said, Look. If you're gonna fight, don't fight on the street. I did and look where the fuck it got me. If you're that fuckin good, go in the ring and make a few bucks, but no more of this shit on the street. One Apt in prison is enough for any family. "

"Kinda like Joe Frazier, my best punch was my left hook. There was a decent boxing gym in Elmwood Park that turned out a couple a pro fighters, so I went down there. They, of course, sorta blew me off and told me to go hit the heavy bag a few times, not expecting much. But when I hit the bag it made a 'Thwack' sound that they hadn't heard before, because they all just kinda stopped and stared at me. Turned out I had a punch and some talent. From there, they had me come in on a regular basis to train me. After about a month, I could box, move my feet with precision, and defend myself."

Ray butts in again, "But man oh man, could he punch!"

"I trained five fuckin days a week. It became everything to me. I trained, listened, paid attention and worked my ass off. It was like an obsession for me. Next thing I know, I'm in the Golden Gloves Tournament boxing at 156 pounds."

"The kid's just sixteen years old and fighting in this huge fuckin tournament, only of course I can't be there and it's killing me. I know he had a picture of me that he hung in locker room which was about as close as I was gonna get. At least I was there in spirit."

Ray, Jr. continues, "So, my first fight is with this Italian kid. Holy Shit. We just went at it throwing bombs at each other for the full three rounds. I was exhausted. I guess I got a few more licks in on him than he got in on me because I won. Only, man it was close. I think I got lucky to win that one."

He takes a sip of his drink. "The next fight was easy, especially compared to the first one. Before I know it, I'm in the goddamn Novice Title fight at 156 pounds, which is a tough fuckin weight class."

Ray excitedly jumps in, "I got it from the same friends of mine who called me in Joliet to tell me my kid was out of control that Junior here just kept throwing bombs at this kid, and the kid he hits ain't even flinching. And now the kid is throwing bombs back at Junior and this keeps going on for the first two rounds."

The two of them were reliving the fight as they were telling me about it.

"With about a minute to go in the third and final round, I get the kid pinned on the back of the ropes and really connect with a solid left, my best shot. I followed that up with six or seven left hooks in a row. Where I got the energy and strength is beyond me, because I'm dyin out there. I then go for broke and hit the kid with a left right combination and still the fuckin kid wouldn't go down."

Ray's pumped up excited hearing his son re-tell this story and jumps in. "So, the final decision goes to the fuckin judges." My friends tell me they're going ape shit!"

"I couldn't believe it. I won in a shocker! No one and I mean no one thought I had a shot at winning the fuckin title. Not even my trainers. I gotta tell ya, all that pain I was feeling went away for a few minutes when they raised my hand. Wow. What a feeling. And I knew that that fight was the beginning of something great for me."

"By the time the kid was 21, he'd fought 70 fights and won seventeen fuckin Golden Gloves titles. You believe that?? Seventeen! I was so fuckin proud of him!!" Ray was beaming.

"I finally went pro at twenty-one and had my first fight as a super middleweight. It lasted a whole twelve seconds. Kinda like that Norton-Bobick fight. The bell rings, I get off my stool, walk out to the middle of the ring and nail the sonofabitch with a left-hand haymaker and dropped him cold right there. The fuckin place went nuts."

Ray, still beaming, "The kid won his first seven fights, just knockin people out or kickin the crap outta them. I started keeping a scrap book on him. And a lotta the inmates were rooting for him, too!"

"Things were going so great, but maybe too great cuz life made a left hand turn on me. One night I'm in the car with my step dad. He's driving and I'm in the passenger seat. My step sister's in the back seat. And it's just fuckin pouring rain. All of sudden, our whole car is like washed over by lights. So, I look back and here's this fuckin truck with a bulldog on its hood barreling down on us about to hit the back of our car. I reach back and put my hand on my step sister to brace her for the impact and BAM! We get hit. And just like that, my arm snaps and breaks my left elbow. That was it for me. That left was my weapon and now it's pretty much worthless. Good thing was we all lived through it. Bad thing was, my life as I knew it was over."

"He went in for some major surgery to repair it, but his fighting days were over for a while."

"Awhile? You kidding? Not just a long fuckin while, more like forever. Obviously, I had to find something else to do."

"Remember when I was talking about decisions we make and being willing to pay the consequences for 'em. Well, this is the part where Junior here made all the wrong ones and was total fuckin idiot."

"My dad was always harping on how you make decisions, you make choices and they're yours... right or wrong... man up and deal with them. Well, just like him, I started making every wrong fuckin decision you can make in life. I started knocking off drug dealers and robbing them of whatever they had. I tossed one off a roof. I never used a weapon, just my fists. And when I hit em, they were out. So, this goes on for about five years and I think I'm doing Ok. Till this one night, my buddy says he spotted an easy mark with a lotta weed and cash. I say's I'm in. So, we drive to where the guy lives and it's a basement apartment. My buddy had set the whole thing up ahead of time so the guy thinks we're there to buy. I knock on the door, he looks at me and says, 'You got the money?' I say, Yeh! And I toss this bag on the table, and it sure as hell LOOKS like a a stack of money, but it's really all fake. I say's, You got the stuff? He points to the closet. I go over the closet and there sits 30 fuckin trash bags full of killer weed. I walk back to the kid, grab him by the neck and slam him against the wall with pictures and shit falling all over the place. I'm yelling at my buddy to grab the fuckin trash bags and get the fuck outta here. Just as I did that, taking my eyes off the drug dealer for just a split second, he pulls out a fuckin knife and stabs me in the head with it. All of a sudden this night is becoming a goddamn nightmare. To make it worse, the fuckin asshole is about to stab me in the head a second time when I grab his hand and bend his arm all the way back to where I can sink my teeth into his finger and bite part of it off. He screams and drops the fuckin knife and now I'm kickin the shit outta him because I'm so pissed off I can't see straight. I wanted to kill that motherfucker. Finally, we get the fuck outta there and go running up the steps, only here comes this short little Domino's pizza guy with his Walkman going coming down the stairs carrying a pizza. He takes one look at us, gets as close to the wall as he can and freezes with his eyes about the size of silver dollars. I still laugh thinking about what he musta seen. I'm bleeding, no I'm literally gushin blood outta my fuckin head carrying fifteen black trash bags of marijuana and a knife. My buddy's got the other fifteen bags. So, as we run by the pizza guy, my buddy grabs the pizza outta the kid's hands, we throw everything inside the car, and we take off."

"Stupid fuckin kid. Coulda been killed. It took 17 stitches inside the gash and 25 more stitches on the outside to close him up. It scared the ever lovin crap outta him, especially seeing all that blood knowing it was his own fuckin blood. He got lucky. He got damn lucky. Kids. Ya can't cut 'em up into little pieces, but there's times you'd like to!"

Ray gives a menacing look towards his son and puts his fist in front of his son's face.

"So, here I am, sixty-two years old and I'm being released from prison on parole. You know, sitting in prison, knowing you gotta son, and that no matter what he does, you can't be there for him is tough. I told you, I made a lotta bad decisions and the worst one was believing that life as a wise guy was more important than being a father. Man, that was probably my worst all time decision because there's a void and it can't ever be filled. Fact is, there's nothing there to fill it with. I wasn't there. I wasn't ever there. Now that's emptiness and that's tough. I will say that now, the more we're around each other the more we grow and understand each other. But it'll never be as it could have been or should have been. I fucked that one up."

"Hey. It's never too late to have a happy childhood."

"Go fuck yourself."

*"Fast is fine but accuracy is final.
You need to learn to be slow in a hurry."* Wyatt Earp

• CHAPTER TWENTY-FIVE •

"Fuck me, Jagoff. Apt spends half his life in prison and still has a relationship with his kid and mine won't even talk to me. What the fuck?!?

"You through?"

"No, asshole."

"Then just keep talking."

"You know your book doesn't tell the half of it."

"Wasn't meant to. I just wanted to immortalize the characters."

"Immortalize?!? You ARE fucking nuts!"

We both laugh.

"I gotta ask you. Why, after over forty fucking years did you decide to finally finish this book?"

"Because I finally had the time and there probably ain't a whole helluvalot of that left."

"Time. Wow. Interesting how some of us have more of that than others."

"Hey. We all had the same amount of time that Alexander the Great, Julius Caesar and Napoleon had."

"Speaking of Napoleon, you interview Elaine? I'd love to know what she has to say."

"Elaine, who?"

"My fucking ex-wife, jagoff."

"How long was Elaine with you?"

"Are you kidding? Elaine was never with me. She was against from the start!"

"Then why'd you marry her?"

"She gave great headache."

"That's bullshit and you know it."

"Yeh, you're probably right." Bill pauses and gets a reflective look on his face.

"I'm telling you, right now, she couldn't warm up to me now if we were cremated together."

"Well, truth be known, I did interview her. You want to read it?"

"What else do I have to do? Sure."

"So, Elaine, what in the hell was it with you and Bill?"

"You know all that Men are from Mars crap that explains the difference between men and women? And it IS crap! Because the only reason men can't understand women is that they've never been one. They have no idea what it's like to get so hooked on a guy that like a fucking dog, you go back to him no matter how rotten he treats you. Ok, so maybe I was just young and stupid just like all women in their twenties are. Or, maybe I was drugged, seduced, stupefied, mesmerized and fucked up. Whatever it was, he had me from the moment I laid eyes on him. The man was like catnip, not just to me, but to most women. What can I say? You can only be young once, but you can be immature and stupid your whole life if you want to be. Truth is that without Devin, Bill would have been my downfall because I'd have never broke away from him. Thank God that Devin did come along."

"Why did you and Bill get married in the first place instead of just living together?"

"Because I got pregnant, remember?"

"Oh, yeh. I forgot that part."

"If that hadn't happened, no we wouldn't have gotten married. I always looked at marriage as a union, much like the United Auto Workers, the SEIU and the Teamsters. No. Marriage wasn't in the plans."

"Did you learn anything from Bill while you were with him?"

"Oh, man, what planet did you just parachute in from? THAT's one helluva loaded question."

Turning a bit red from embarrassment, "Yeh, you got me on that one."

"I'll say. Other than drugs and great sex, Bill taught me that the toughest year of any marriage is the one you're in. He also taught me that you should always follow your heart, but that never meant, leave your brains behind, because I sure did when it came to him."

"Ok, so now, how bad did things get?"

"Hold on numb-nuts. Before you start asking me about how bad things got, let's talk about how good things were at first."

"Ok, so what positive things did you see in Bill when you first started dating him?"

"He had drugs. He was charming. He had drugs. He was handsome. He had drugs. He was fun to be with. He had drugs. He had money. He had drugs. He was always living on the edge. And, he had drugs."

"So, you knew he was a drug dealer when you first hooked up with him."

Looking more than a bit incredulous and letting out a laugh, "Are you kidding? I used as much or more coke than he did! Plus, there was always our honeymoon. Ah, yeh, I think it was pretty clear to me that he was a drug dealer."

Anything else to say about him that was positive?

"Sure. One thing with Bill is that he was consistent. The only time he'd do the right thing was when he was cornered, or someone had him in handcuffs. And the other thing with Bill is that Bill either promised you everything and then forgot about it as fast as he said it, or he promised you nothing, and boy did he deliver."

"Tell me about you and Bill once Devin arrived."

"First off, I got pregnant on a fuckin diaphragm if you can believe that?!? So much for how well they work! "

"So, you and Bill were not looking to have a kid."

"Wow. I'm impressed. You actually figured that out all by yourself and without a computer! Are you kidding? Me and Bill PARENTS!! Both of us together were about as rock solid as Jello."

"You ever consider an abortion?"

"That was my first thought, but my second thought changed it. I'd already had two abortions and decided enough was enough. We're keeping this kid no matter what."

"Pretty big decision."

"It was. Bill and I talked it over and figured that with the support of the grandparents, we should be able to pull this off. I mean it was a lot more responsibility than buying a pitcher of beer at a bar, or bringing a dog home from the pound."

"Did you think Bill was the worst person in the world?"

"Hey. The world's a big place. All I can say is that he was the worst person in my world."

"Was he a shitty husband?"

"No. He wasn't abusive or hard to get along with. We had fun and the sex was great."

"So?"

"Well, you know how selfish and self-centered Bill is and how he would always put himself, his needs and his wants ahead of anyone else's, including mine."

"So?"

"I was fine with it until we became parents. Bill was a shitty father which, changed everything."

"Do you think Bill THOUGHT he was a good a husband and father?"

"I think Bill figured as long as he wasn't doing a lot of the bad things a lotta other husbands were doing, and was taking care of things financially, he thought that's all he needed to do."

"Did you talk to him?"

"You know him. Did he listen? C'mon, it's Bill for Crissakes. He can justify anything and even rationalize it to where it sounds right even when I know what I'm hearing is pure bullshit."

"You guys fight?"

"You mean scream, yell, get angry, tell him he's crazy and call him fucking names? Sure."

"What do you think was the critical issue that caused the downfall between you and Bill?"

"Hey. Anyone who knows Bill, knows how irresponsible he is. I mean the guy never really held a job in his life."

"So, are there any examples to share?"

"How much time you got?"

"Plenty."

"Here's a perfect example. I have a meeting to attend and leave Bill to watch Devin. I'm gone no more than ten minutes and he sends me an SOS on the pager letting me know there's an emergency. I turn the car around, tear back home, fly up the stairs and there's Devin sleeping on Bill's chest. I ask him what the fuck? He says he wanted to get up to grab a beer but when he did the baby woke up and it freaked him out."

"And you said?"

"It's what babies fucking do!! He was so fucking clueless!"

"Did he ever help with anything?"

"We are talking about Bill, right? He didn't even give excuses. He just didn't wanna. And if ya don't wanna, guess what? You ain't gonna do it. And whenever he actually managed to do something helpful, he wanted a goddamn standing ovation and a monument built to him every time he did."

Elaine fires up a cigarette and takes a deep drag. "Another thing that really pissed me off is that if me, Bill and Devin go to a party or even White's, you'd swear he's Robert Young, Hugh Beaumont, Ozzie Nelson and Father of the Year all wrapped up in one."

"Sounds like Bill."

"You know, I gotta believe he tried, but like so many other things he's done with his life, he failed."

"What's the worst he would do?"

"Neglect Devin. I mean if it were convenient for Bill, he'd play with Devin and pay attention to him. But, if it wasn't convenient for Bill, or you caught him at a bad time, he'd just leave him unsupervised which sometimes proved dangerous."

"Like?"

"Like when he crawled out of the apartment and…"

"Are we talking about Bill or Devin?"

"Cute. Devin. He crawls out of the apartment unnoticed by Bill and heads for the stairs."

"Oh, shit."

"Yeh, oh, shit. Thank God the neighbor grabbed him."

"I always tried to imagine Bill disciplining Devin, but never could."

"Because he wouldn't. Shit, he can't discipline himself much less Devin."

"Did you consider yourself Mother of the Year?"

"Oh, fuck no. Bill and I used drugs right in front of Devin. We'd roll joints, snort a line of blow. It didn't really hit me until that day I watched Devin grab a straw and try to snort the cigarette ashes out of the ash tray. That was a wakeup call for me."

"Wow!"

"Wow is right. Bill was right there with me, but it never registered on him. But again, it was Bill."

She pulls another drag on her cigarette. "I really think Bill thought he was the perfect husband, and we just went on pretending that everything was okay when in fact it wasn't.

He truly stopped being the perfect husband when he'd get up around noon or one, leave the house around three, and stay out all night leaving it on me not to just take care of Devin, pay all the bills, buy the groceries, handle all the problems, everything. I think he just figured my parents would do the heavy lifting so he didn't have to."

Elaine takes another deep drag on the cigarette and crushes it in the nearby ashtray.

"And it wasn't like he was cheating, which he may have been considering that when it came to women, Bill was pretty much like a roving dog who couldn't be kept on the porch. But what it really came down to was really Bill's lack of commitment. You have to understand that feelings came and went with Bill and in looking back, I have to believe he was in love with the idea of love, but that was about it."

Elaine turns away to think for a moment, then turns back.

"Commitment for Bill was pretty much faking feelings that had long disappeared. And like I said, everything changed with the arrival of Devin."

"You once told me that you could always make another Devin, but you couldn't find another Bill."

"I actually remember saying that to you in White's. And now you know how fucking stupid I was back then."

"You have any regrets?"

"About Bill? No. Resentment, yes, but no regrets. It was a great ride while it lasted and then I got to raise Devin without him. No. No regrets."

"When did you decide to file for divorce."

"When I realized I didn't need a roommate. I needed a friend, and I needed a husband. I didn't need someone who just came home, ate, slept and left. I wanted someone who would be a part of the whole process. I truly needed a husband, and he was just incapable of being that person."

"Anything more you want to add?"

"Yes. I have no doubt that Bill was the absolute right guy for me before we had Devin. But once we became parents, or should I say I became a parent, and Bill just continued on like before, it all unraveled. And as I said, I was a shitty mother at first because I tried hanging on to the lifestyle I had and loved. Only, I grew up enough to realize you can't do that when you have this little human being you're responsible for and who is completely dependent on you."

"Anything else?"

"Yeh. There was a time that Bill told me that I'd miss him when he was gone, and I'd see what a great husband and father he really was."

"What did you say to that?"

"I told him he should drop dead now so me and Devin could put his statement to the test."

"Ring tailed Tom on the fence, old pussy cat on the ground, Ring Tailed Tom took that pussy cat and they went rambling round. Lord he's quick on the trigger, he's a natural born crack shot. He's got a new target every night and he sure does practice a lot." Scottish Folksong

• CHAPTER TWENTY-SIX •

So, let's get fourteen tons of bituminous coal heavy here."

"Now what in the fuck are you talking about?"

"May 10, 1985 in Whites"

"What about it?"

"Let me read to you what I've written based on what I've come to know."

Bill Ott walked over to where Raffin and Ronnie Williams were sitting and orders them both a drink.

"Hey, Betty. Three cocktails over here!"

Just then the phone rings and Betty answers it.

"White's! I said, WHITE'S! This is who, lookin for what? Oh, Otto!" Bill looks at Betty and shakes his head no.

"No, he ain't here. Both Ronnie Williams and Raffin are though. What? Yeh. Their kids go to that school."

Betty turns to Ronnie Williams. "Say, Ronnie, they want to talk to you. It's someone from the grade school looking for parents. I guess Mr. Ott gave them this number to call."

Ronnie looks at Betty before grabbing the phone. "What the fuck? Why don't they call Vicki? She deals with all that disrupting the class shit he does, not me."

Betty holds the phone out for Ronnie. "They sound serious."

"Hello. Yeh, I'm Ronnie Williams. Yeh, my kid's name is Donny. What he do.... WHAT!?! No fuckin' WAY!! I'll be right there!!" Ronnie looks ashen.

Raffin gives Ronnie a serious look. "What the fuck happened?"

"C'mon, we gotta go! The school bus crashed and all the kids were taken to Gottlieb Memorial. It's bad. They think some kids were killed. Let's go!! "

I start the recorders and look back to Bill.

"Now let me read you the Tribune's coverage starting with the headline.

'Driver Blamed in School Bus Crash.' From there the story goes:
'The school bus crash that killed one River Grove sixth-grader as well as the bus driver, while injuring 14 others was apparently caused by 'driver error' on the part of the driver.

The bus crash occurred about 3:30pm when the driver lost control of the bus and struck a telephone pole near the intersection of Oak Street and Grand Avenue, in River Grove. All survivors of the crash were immediately taken to Gottlieb Memorial Hospital for examination. The dead youngster was identified as Ricky Raffin, Jr. The bus driver was Joe Rogus.

Preliminary investigation of the May 10th crash, in which the bus rammed into the telephone pole, has proved that the bus was mechanically sound.

According to Frank Dallas of the Department of Public Safety, 'As of this moment, I have not found anything wrong with the vehicle that would have caused this accident."

"All of you were in White's that day that included you, Ronnie Williams, Raffin, Macatelli, and most everyone. But then the phone rang and everything changed for all of you."

"You weren't there. So, what the fuck do you know?"

"I don't know."

"There's a lotta things you don't know."

I push the recorders closer to Bill. "As I said, your whole world and everything changed that day. Devin, your own son got pretty banged up on that bus fifteen years ago. As did Ronnie's and Mac's kids. Raffin stopped hanging around with you guys completely after his kid, Ricky, Jr. was killed in the crash. And now, you're in here for having sold Rogus, who was driving the bus, the drugs he was on when he plowed into that tree. Not to mention that Rogus also died in the crash."

"Yeh, what about it?"

"You never hired a lawyer and you defended yourself in court. Devin wanted nothing to do with you and Elaine stopped talking to you."

"What was there to defend. I did it. Guilty as charged."

"Were you?"

"What's with you? It was my turn in the barrel. Besides, what the fuck difference does it make?"

"Was it your turn in the barrel? Or, should it have been someone else's turn?"

"Where you going with all of this?"

"I was sitting in White's long after you went to prison and Elaine comes in."

"So?"

"So, here's the conversation between Elaine and Betty as I heard it."

"Elaine, you hear that Bill is getting out soon?"

"Out? Out of what?"

"Prison."

"No."

"He should be out in a few weeks."

"Ok, so Bill's getting out and coming back to DO what? Be angry, kill me, take vengeance on the world? What? He can't go back to selling drugs. So, you gonna put him to work here at the bar?"

"Now that's a great idea. I'll hire him as a bartender so he can look you right in the eye every time he pours you a drink."

"You do that!"

"You gonna pick him up at the front gate when he gets out?"

Then Ronnie Williams jumps into the conversation.

"Betty, where you going with all this crap?"

"Where I'm going with all this crap is that it wasn't Bill who got Joe Rogus so loaded that he plowed that school bus into a tree, it was Mrs. Ott here and she damn well knows it! "

"Fuck, you!"

Betty, ignoring Elaine's retort, "It wasn't Bill who killed Raffin's kid and injured all the others! It isn't Bill who should be in jail, it should be you, because you're the one who got

Joe loaded, not Bill!"

"You got no proof of that!! If you did, I'd be in jail and not Bill. And if they had the proof back then, fifteen fucking years ago, I'd be in jail and not Bill. Fuck you and fuck your bar!"

"So, Betty, what proof do you have? Remember, my kid was on that bus, too."

A red faced and seething Elaine, still seated at the bar chimes in, "She ain't got dick! That's exactly what she's got!!"

"Well, Betty?"

"Elaine, c'mon, as a mother. You mean to tell me your conscience hasn't bothered you for all these years? It doesn't bother you to know you had a hand in killing Raffin's kid and injuring fourteen others, including your own son?"

"It can't bother me if I didn't do it!"

"Betty, so where's your proof. So far, it's just a bunch of fucking conjecture and superfluous jargon."

"Hold on Ronnie, I'm getting there."

"Hold on to what?"

"Elaine, you had your own husband take the rap for you and that doesn't bother you?"

"Bother me? You kiddin? Selling drugs was our business. It's how we made our money. But the bus crash was all Bill's fault. Everything traced back to him, not me! Bill's the one who got sloppy with the sales. He's the one who kept using more than he sold. He's the one who fucked up our business. He's the one whose big fuckin mouth and loose ways of doing things got the feds sniffing around us. He's the one who took us from running shit through

O'Hare Airport to staying small time. He's the one who couldn't take the pressure and he proved that when he caved in court. He's the one who fucked up, not me!"

"Holy Shit! You framed him to get the fuck rid of him!!"

"That's it. I'm outta here."

"Hold on, Elaine", Ronnie says as he grabs her arm. "This is beginning to get interesting."

"What!?! You're now buying into her crap?"

"Don't know. Still waiting for her to show me some proof."

"Fuck the two of you. There never was any proof and there ain't none now!"

Now Macatelli enters the conversation. "Elaine, I never thought of this before, but YOU were a whole lot closer to Joe Rogus than Bill ever was. Come to think of it, Bill didn't even like Joe Rogus, so why would Joe go to Bill when he was used to dealing with you?"

"Oh, for God's sake!" says Elaine, glaring at Betty. "See what you started?!? Now you got all these mutants riled up about nothing!! It must hurt to be this stupid!"

"C'mon, Elaine, fess up. Why is it that right after Devin was released from the hospital, you took off for your farm in Wisconsin and stayed up there never showing up for the trial? And why is it that when the cops questioned you about Joe Rogus, you put them on Bill's trail to get them off you?"

"You're full a shit!"

"Did you set Bill up to take the fall? And did you kill Raffin's kid and Joe Rogus?"

"Killed? What killed?!? "

"I think you did, mom."

"Devin!! Where the fuck did YOU come from?"

"Betty called me and asked me to come. I slipped in the back door and heard the whole conversation."

"Well, you're as fucked up as the rest of these assholes. "

"Am I?"

"And just how the fuck do you even know Betty?"

"Mom, I'm 23. I've been drinking in here for the past four-years!. She's been pumping me, and a whole bunch of other people for information for a long time now. She even visited dad in Joliet and sat with Raffin a bunch of times. Joe Rogus' wife, too."

Jesus! Ain't you got anything better to do with your life, Betty? And, come to think of it, why in the fuck do even care?"

"Because Joe Rogus was my first cousin. Because Joe Rogus was a good guy and will forever be remembered for driving that bus into a tree. Because my entire family is fucked up over it and Thanksgiving dinner has never been the same since. That's why."

Betty throws a bar rag and walks to the other end of the bar to cool off.

"Mom, you got any idea what it's like to have you and dad as a parents? You got any idea what it's like to have your friends ask, *So, what's your dad do? Oh, he sells drugs for a living. Need any?* Your entire fucking lives were one missed opportunity after another. Look at you! What direction did you and dad ever give me other than sports? Growing up you taught me that you don't really need to work for anything or take orders from anyone. Then I grew up to find that was all bullshit!"

"Devin, I'm sorry. I fucked up. No, we fucked up. I'm sorry."

"Sorry!?! Are you kidding me?!? Fuck you, sorry. You and dad had more opportunities to make something of yourself that I ever did. And look what you both did with 'em. Nothing! And worse, you guys didn't just walk away from them, you spit on 'em and crushed 'em like a cockroach or shit on your shoes."

"Look me in the fuckin' eye and tell me you think I'm guilty."

"I'll not only look you in the eye, I'll spit in it."

Elaine looks down and stares at her drink.

"You know, Mom. It doesn't matter if it was you or dad who was responsible for getting Rogus wasted because you were both in it together. You both always lived on the edge and lived for the excitement. I guess I have more of *your* dad in my genes than I do either you or dad because, yeh, I enjoy getting high every now and then, but not like you two."

"Where you going?"

"Anywhere but here." Devin turns his back on Elaine and heads out the door.

• CHAPTER TWENTY-SEVEN •

"You made that up."

"Almost wish I had, but it really happened."

"Have to say, Devin's right. What difference does it make which one of us sold Rogus the drugs? And actually, if Rogus hadn't died, they'd never have come after me. I mean, no one forced him to take the drugs. But with him dead, they had to hang it on somebody."

"Did Elaine really set you up to get rid of you?"

"No, not at all. We agreed she needed to be with Devin, not me. Could you imagine me raising Devin? Truth be known, I can't even take care of myself, much less Devin. He'd have turned out worse than me."

"So, he got the best of the worst."

"Hey, Elaine did the best she could with what she had. It's now up to Devin to make something of himself, or not, and get over the 'poor me' bullshit."

"I'm sure he will."

"You remember when we were kids and the fucking government, some House Committee on Juvenile Delinquency came to the brilliant conclusion that comic books made kids juvenile delinquents?"

"Oh, yeah! We were babies when the hearings actually took place, but yeh, I remember that bullshit."

"Well, I'm here to tell you I'm the only one of the group who read comic books."

"I remember you had a huge collection of Superman."

"Apt, no. John Bree, no. Brian King, no. And most everyone else I knew, NO, except YOU who read Mad Magazine and fucking Pogo!"

"Your point?"

"My point is that Devin can't blame me, or Elaine, or his circumstances, or comic books for how he turns out. We each figure out our own paths and take 'em. I always took the wrong ones, but they were my choices, and I certainly didn't take them because I was influenced by fucking comic books."

"How about movies?"

"What about them?"

"I recall you loved the movie White Heat with James Cagney. 'Look, Ma! I'm on top of the world!'"

"That was a great movie. And yeh, I kind of related to it."

"You ever make it to the top of the world?"

"Does this look like it?" Bill opens his arms and points to the inside of the prison.

"But I do have to say, I did hit it big. I really was a big shot for a while. Only no one ever stays on top forever."

"Wow, Bill, you really are a realist."

"Hey. My race is over and I finished out of the money, but there were those times I hit the board big. Not everyone can say that."

"No argument from me."

"I've always believed that impermanence is not only a fact of life, but that nobody gets out of this game of life alive."

"You're beginning to sound like Ray Apt."

"Who's he?" Bill asked smiling.

"I brought you a short story to read. Thought you could relate to it."

"What is it?"

"The Hunger Artist by Kafka."

"You're getting pretty heavy aren't you?"

"Just read it."

• CHAPTER TWENTY-EIGHT •

"Mr. Ott. You have a visitor."

"Me? Who?"

"Raymond Apt."

"No fucking way."

"You want to see him or not?"

"Yeh, I'll see him."

"Hi, Bill."

"Raymond. Holy Shit, we got old."

"Yeh, we did. So, tell me, how you holding up in here?"

"The service sucks, but other than that, I got no complaints."

"From what I understand, maybe you shouldn't even be in here."

"I think you've been fed some false information. I most certainly belong in here."

"I hear Devin paid you a visit."

"He did."

"I also heard that you told him you were better off in prison than out because you couldn't hurt anyone you love as long as you were in prison and that you didn't have the balls to commit suicide."

"Yeh, so?"

"Here's how I see things. Each of us is the architect of our own lives and each of us is the final product. The problem though, is that to truly become who you are, you have to begin with the end, or what they call *Respice Finem*. And there always is an end because we are all mortal, which is why in Rome they used to have a guy chasing after Julius Caesar yelling *Memento Mori, Remember you are Mortal*."

"Ray, you read too much."

"Prison gave me a lot of time to think and read and what I figured out is that I blew it. I never thought about the future and where I was headed, only about today. But the more I thought about it, the more I realized that the future is not some invisible place and only remains invisible until I start thinking about it."

"Ray, I don't have a future, so why should I give a fuck?"

"Because everything is temporary, even this place. Impermanence is a fact of life and so is finitude. And so is interdependence. Things not only change, but they also end. And everything we do eventually affects someone or something because nothing we do is done in a vacuum."

"Where are you going with all of this?"

"First off, as Will Durant once wrote, 'Civilization exists by geological consent, subject to change without notice'. The vast majority of people haven't a clue that there are tectonic plates and the earth continues to shift a couple of inches every year. Did you ever stop to think that over a span of a billion years that that comes to about 67,000 miles?"

"Ray, you never cease to amaze me."

"Do you know what makes this 4.567 billion-year-old planet different from all the other planets?"

"Not a clue."

"Constant change and reinvention. Right now, the Pacific Ocean is shrinking, the Atlantic Ocean is expanding, Mt. Everest is getting taller, the Appalachians continue to shrink, India continues to move into China and Los Angeles, California is moving two inches a year toward San Francisco."

"You said the earth is how old?"

"4.567 billion. And it hasn't always looked like it does now. Even before the growth of continents and land masses could occur, granite had to be created from peridotite and basalt. Then came tectonic plates that have caused continents to be on the move since their creation. It started with Kenorland, Laurentia, Gonwanda, Columbia, Rodinia, and Pangea to name but a few. You have any idea why there are four active volcanoes in the Northwest United States?"

"I haven't a clue."

"Because of Columbia." Barely taking breath, Ray keeps going. "There was an ocean named Iapetus that separated the great Appalachian mountains on North America's East Coast from the great Appalachian mountains in Scotland. And where Iapetus once sat, the Atlantic now sits and continues to expand.

"You already told me that."

Ignoring Bill, Ray continues, "Do you have any idea how the moon was formed?"

Looking bored, Bill responds, "No, but I'm sure you're about to enlighten me."

"There was the Great Thwack when Theia smashed into Earth taking a chunk of Earth along with it to form the Moon. And the moon itself was once a lot closer to earth than it is now. Plus, it's still moving away from us. Or take the sun. It didn't give off the same heat it does now. Or the oceans that began with iron then sulfur because oxygen didn't exist until much later. Yet there were still single cell organisms living in it. And all that changed as a result of the 'Great Oxidation Event' causing Earth to change forever. You have any idea how long it takes an ocean to become oxygenated?"

"Have to say I've never given it a thought, Ray."

"A billion fucking years!"

"Ray. Take it easy. You're getting overheated."

"Did you know there have been some three to five mass extinctions since life began where at least thirty percent of every species living on land, in the sea or in the air became extinct?"

"Can't say that I did."

"For that matter, some ninety-nine percent of every species that ever existed on Earth are extinct."

"Are you serious or just making this shit up?"

Ray gives Bill a look. "Ok. You're serious, but again, where you going with this?"

"Where I'm going is that death should remind us that existence cannot be postponed. The point is that us humans, who like every other man-like species before us will be replaced by yet another species. Before Homo Sapiens there was Homo Erectus. Before that Homo Habilis. Before that Neanderthal. Something will eventually replace us. But as long as we're here, we attempt to make our mark and leave our mark. Let me ask you this. Do you know what the definition of a species is?"

"Yeh. A categorized living being."

"Not quite. It's a categorized living being that is guaranteed to one day become extinct and be replaced by something else. Unfortunately, for most of us, we merely pass and are forgotten with the rest. It's pretty much why we have kids and build monuments to ourselves."

"Or, as Walt Kelly once wrote, "Don't take life none too serious, cuz it ain't no how permanent.""

Ignoring Bill's comment, Ray continued, "You know why we measure time in minutes, hours, days, weeks, months, years, and decades instead of eons, millions and billions of years?"

"I give up."

"Because we truly believe that homo-sapiens are the ultimate creation superior to all else."

"Aren't we?"

"To believe that is to deny evolution. No. Something will eventually replace us."

"Like I said, Ray. I don't have a future and I probably don't have a lot of time left."

"You ever read The Killers by Hemingway?"

"You mean that movie where they rob a racetrack?"

"No. That was The Killing. This is The Killers about a guy who just sits and accepts his fate."

"So, enlighten me."

"There's this heavyweight fighter who pissed off the mob and of course they were out to bump him off."

"Right up your alley, Ray."

Ignoring the comment, Apt continues. "So finally, the guy gets tired of running, sits in his dingy apartment and just waits for these two guys who are sitting in a coffee shop to bump him off. The mark has resigned himself to his fate, and accepted the inevitable just like you're doing."

Bill scrunches his nose up, shakes his head and looks at Ray. "I don't know if I'm buying that." Bill gets a contemplative look and stares back at Ray.

"You ever read The Hunger Artist by Kafka?"

"Can't say that I have."

"It's about this guy who starves himself to death."

"Oh, so now you're gonna play Ghandi?"

"No, asshole. It's a story about a make believe spectator sport where the contestants starve themselves to death. People pay to watch them do this and bet on who will die first and who will last the longest. The Hunger Artist is like the Muhammad Ali of this sport. Only after a while, people lost interest in the sport and ignored the guy. The sport becomes passé and the people could now care less if he starved himself to death or not. So, they move the guy from where he is to a circus cage, only even at the circus no one takes any interest in him or the sport. But he keeps it up anyway because it's the only thing he knows how to do. He doesn't know to do anything else."

"And let me guess. The guy dies as in Finitude."

"It's not quite that simple. Yeh. He starves himself to death only nobody ever saw him do it. Turns out one of the circus people see this empty cage and figures they can put a panther in it. Everyone forgot what the cage had been used for and who was in it. So, when they go in to clean it out, they find his dead, emaciated body buried under a bunch of straw. Then they remove the cadaver and stick this panther in there, that is not only happier than a pig in shit to be in the cage, but loves to eat!"

"Your point."

"My point is that the Hunger Artist, even as a has been... even long after his career was over, kept up the act to the bitter end. He just had a need to perform even when no one wanted to see it or cared about it. It's all he knew. So, in the end, he just disappears and no one even notices."

"And that's you?"

"Yeh. I was somebody once. And like him, I'm gonna just disappear and no one is gonna remember I was ever here, much less notice I'm gone."

"Let me ask you this. You ever think about the idea of eternal re-occurrence?"

"How can I think about something that I don't even know what the fuck it is?"

"Ok. So, instead of an afterlife, or instead of reincarnation, what if you had to relive every moment of your life, just as it was, with all the joy, pain, ecstasy, agony, hurt, disappointments, thrills, suffering, and everything else included, over and over and over again. Like Ground Hog Day, only nothing can change."

"What's the question?"

"If you knew in advance that eternal reoccurrence was your fate, how would you have lived your life and would it be different than the life you lived? And that includes all the decisions you made, all the choices you made, all the paths you took, and all the doors you opened and walked through, knowing you'd be reliving the consequences for all of them forever?"

"You know damn well I wouldn't have lived the life I lived if that had been the case, but fortunately for both of us, asshole, it ain't the case."

"Indulge me in this. You've found Jesus, or so you say. So, do you live your life in fear of having to meet your Maker, or do you live a life full of good values and high morals because of who you are?"

"Yeh, I've found Jesus and I know I'm gonna pay the price for what I've done. So, yes. I've resigned myself to God sending me to Hell."

"Then let me change the question. What if everything you did and the way you did it throughout your life became universal law for everyone else to follow? What if everything you did in life set the standard for everyone else to follow?"

"I'd say there'd be a lot more fucked up people out there than there already are, and the world would be even more of a mess than it is. So, again, where in the fuck are you going with this, since you're even more fucked up than I am?"

"We're two peas in a pod, Bill. Neither of us can truly say that the lives we lived were thrust upon us. We both welcomed the lives we lived with open arms. Ever since my dad threw me into the wall, I've always known who I am, but I'm not so sure you have."

"Ray, you're full of shit."

"You familiar with the Myth of Sisyphus?"

"Yeh. The guy stuck rolling a rock up and down a hill forever."

"The story is that he was dead but was allowed to go back to earth to get even with his wife. Only, once back on earth he didn't want to go back to being dead."

"Can you blame him?"

"No. Only the gods had had enough of his bullshit, so they sent Mercury to drag his ass back to the kingdom of the dead and punish him by pushing that rock up the hill."

"I never knew that."

"Most people don't. And, what most people don't understand is that Sisyphus made the best of his bad situation. Instead of cursing his lot in life and seeing his misfortune as an accident of sorts, he saw it as a lesson meant to teach him something he needed to learn. He not only took full responsibility for what happened to him without blaming anyone else, but he looked upon it as an opportunity to learn."

"I swear, Ray. You should've been a teacher."

"You know what was one of the first things he discovered?"

"No, but I'm sure you're gonna tell me."

"It was that the rock not only had a relation with itself, as well as with him and him with the rock, but that the rock was relational to every pebble, blade of grass, insect, plant, animal, hole, and clump of dirt it encountered on the way up and down. What Sisyphus discovered is that everything, you me, the planets, the galaxy and the entire universe are all relational and interdependent. With each trip up that hill, Sisyphus became wiser and more knowledgeable about that mountain and that fucking rock. Instead of bitching and moaning, he became an expert when it came to that mountain and just how that rock would react to it. He came to know every blade of grass on that mountain, every slope, every angle, every hole, every crevice, every pebble, and knew exactly how the rock would react when placed at a certain angle, in a certain place whether going up or down that mountain. He embraced both the rock and the mountain."

"So?"

"So. So is that by learning more about the rock and the mountain he gained insight and knowledge about himself, something you have never had the balls to do."

"Like, you have!"

"Yes, I have. And yes, I do what I do for a living and like Sisyphus, the more I hone my skills, improve my trade and continue to learn, I gain insight to myself and knowledge about who I am."

"Ray, let me ask you. How tall are you, 6 one, 6 two?"

"Bill, what in the fuck do you care how tall I am?"

"Because I never knew they could pile bullshit that high!"

Not missing a beat, Ray continues. "It's not bullshit, Bill. Look. By your not understanding yourself, not knowing your own nature, not taking the necessary time to determine your personal chief aim in life, you've wound up living an ungrounded and wasted life."

"That's your opinion."

"Maybe so, but it sure holds water, doesn't it?"

"Maybe."

"Bill, remember when you were a kid and someone asked you 'What do you wanted to be when you grow up?' What was your response?"

"Like every kid, a policeman, fireman, bank president, rich by the time I'm 30, all the usual bullshit. Why?"

"Because I'm willing to bet you never thought about the real you and what it was you really wanted or what drove you?"

"Ray, I was a fucking kid. How in the fuck am I supposed to know?"

"Because Bill, you're a fully grown adult and you still don't know."

"Point taken."

"How often in life do we all say, 'I just want to be happy'?"

"A lot. Plus, it's a right granted to all in the Constitution."

"No, it's not. It's the *pursuit* of happiness that is. The problem is that most people see happiness as a commodity, wrapped up like a fucking Christmas present, waiting to be found by anyone who has the wherewithal to find it. And then, when the damn thing IS found, it's gone in an instant."

"Now where you going?"

"Bill, your life is the most perfect example I can think of for where I'm going. Your entire life has been wrapped around desire, to satisfaction and right back to desire again. Which is why happiness for you and for most people for that matter is fleeting and temporary."

"So, bright boy, what's the answer to finding it?"

"In the things that drive you! You find happiness in your passions. Passions can make you forget about yourself and can make time literally stand still."

"I'm not sure I'm buying into this. For example, let's say I wasn't born with the advantages some others were born with. Or I was born Black. Or, I was born short, or sickly, or whatever?"

"Ok, I'll give you that. But give me this.... Each of us is born with advantages, disadvantages, certain aptitudes, certain IQs, as well as physical and mental strengths, weaknesses and disabilities. Yes, some are born healthier than others. The challenge is to make the best out of what you were given."

"That's bullshit. Let's say I'm a fifteen-year-old black kid on the West Side of Chicago living in Cabrini Green."

"I don't care who you are, male or female, where you were born, what color you are, or where you're living, each and every one of us arrive in this world with inherent gifts. As humans, each of us has a nature about us. Each of us has limits and potentials. Then, for whatever reason, we spend the first half of our lives abandoning them or letting others disillusion us about them. As young people, we are surrounded by expectations that may have little to do with who we really are. Too often, the expectations of us are held by people who are not trying to discern who we really are, but to fit us into slots. And all too often, it is their slots they are trying to fit us in. In the case of that fifteen-year-old black kid living in Cabrini Green, you can bet that he's being told every day what he OUGHT to be doing, which is probably joining a gang, dealing, stealing, and killing someone. If that kid is fortunate enough to make it to the second half of his life, he's going to spend it trying to recover from the first half and reclaim the gift or gifts he once had."

"Do you really believe life works that way?"

"Bill, we all have something to offer. Ability determines what you can do. Aptitude determines what you can learn to do. Aspiration determines what you hope to do. And attitude determines what you believe you can do. But passion determines what you want to do!"

"Somehow I just knew you'd get back to that."

"Look. Anyone who seeks out a life without understanding who they are and their own nature – their own limitations, capabilities and potential – they place themselves on the road to possible failure by putting themselves in life situations that their nature is not meant to handle. Much like a certain material is meant for specific applications, only. Should you use the material in an application it was not meant for and the material is doomed to failure."

"You saying I'm a failure?"

"No. Only you can determine that. I'm saying I'm a failure. Look, our deepest calling in life is to grow into our own authentic true self, whether or not it conforms to some image of who we, or someone else thinks we OUGHT to be. In other words, by not knowing and understanding who we are, we can go through life wearing one or any number of false masks. We fall prey to what some philosophical men call *Oughtiveness*. 'You know what you ought to do?' 'You know what you ought to be?' 'You really ought to....' You become what someone or even yourself has convinced yourself, you ought to be, instead of what you really are. Which is exactly what I did."

"What *you* did?!? And here I thought you were ragging on me, you fucking jagoff!!"

"What I'm trying to get across to that pig headed brain of yours is that by each of us as individuals, living life in our own way and not the way we think others want us to can you, me, or anyone else be complete. Being successful and achieving things only implies that we like ourselves. That we like what we do and like how we do it. The problem is that success is *NOT* the key to happiness. Happiness is the key to success. Happiness, fulfillment, or better yet, *flourishing* as Aristotle described it allows one to achieve the word he coined, *Eudaimonia*."

"Ray, can you give me just one example of someone who actually did all this crap you're talking about?"

"Yes, and it wasn't all that long ago that he was front page news. Ricky Williams for one and Todd Marinovich for another."

"The Heisman Ricky Williams?"

"Yeh."

"And who?"

"Marinovich. Quarterback for USC and the Raiders. He had all the talent only to realize playing QB really wasn't who he was."

"Oh, he was the kid on heroin. I remember him."

"I always thought of him as the John Stuart Mill of Football."

"What?!?"

"They had the same type of obsessive father."

Bill gives Ray a quizzical look.

"Forget it. It's over your head."

"Don't insult me. I'm sensitive you jag off."

Ignoring Bill's feigned hurt, Ray continues, "I think those two may be the perfect examples of someone finding themselves, while at the top of their professions, and realizing that's not who they were or who they wanted to be."

"I thought Ricky Williams was just a pothead and Marinovich took the stairway to oblivion."

"Far from it. Check out both of them. Both had interesting lives and both are even today, quite an interesting story that more people than just you should know about, Mr. Hunger Artist."

"Ray, is this some kind of catharsis for you, or what?"

"No. I'm just saying that by not understanding who you are, not knowing your own nature, not taking the necessary time to determine your personal chief aim in life, one winds up living an ungrounded life. As a result, just like I did, you can go through life portraying yourself as someone you're really not, based upon the misconception that this is the someone you think you ought to be, when in fact you really aren't that person at all. And in the case of Ricky Williams and Todd Marinovich, they made that discovery early on before they'd lived a life that wasn't them."

I think I've had enough of all this philosophizing, Ray. I gotta headache."

"You ever hear of McAnnula?"

"Did he play for the Sox?"

"Yeh. He was right there with Luke Appling, Mike Kreevich, and Zeke 'Banana Nose' Bonura."

"Wow, Ray. I'm impressed. You know your White Sox! Ok, so what's with McAnnula?"

"He said, *'It is perfectly all right to try to be everything you cannot be when you find that you cannot be everything that you are.'*"

"He drinks, he smokes, he philosophizes and I'll be 85 by the time you get to the fucking point!!"

Ignoring Bill's barb, Ray continues, "According to Erich Fromm, *'Man's main task in life is to give birth to himself, to become what he potentially is.'* But you, like so many others, do nothing but run, never allowing yourself to reflect on where you're running to or what you're running for. Life goes on no matter what we do, but personal growth and development happen only if we allow it to happen and then choose wisely."

"I already told you, I'm the Hunger Artist."

"Bill, it all comes down to *Belief follows need*. What we see and how we interpret what we see confirms what we believe. And, what we believe shapes what we see. Right or wrong, true or false, we believe those things we need to believe in order to support our beliefs. Do I believe what I believe because of what has been instilled in me, or do I believe what I believe because of who I am? I firmly believe that by being aware of who I am, I am far more aware of what I truly believe."

"Go on."

"To lead a life of awareness and authenticity, means being conscious of who we are, what we are doing, why we are acting or reacting the way we are and knowing we are a particle of energy that helps comprise that ocean of energy called Life! Simply stated, what we are is determined by what we think. What we think is often a result of what we've experienced.

Our experiences are based upon those things to which we are exposed. And the experiences we expose ourselves to are based upon who we are."

"Ok. I get it."

"Let me ask you this. Have you ever heard the expression you are what you eat?"

"Oh, brother. Can we end this conversation?"

"I don't know about you, but I am certainly not what I eat. I am not a peanut butter and jelly sandwich! What I eat is determined by who I am. I am not my job, nor am I my life's situations, and I am not my experiences. I have the job I have, I do what I do, I have the experiences I have, and I have the life situations I have because of who I am."

"It's time, Ray. I'm calling the guard."

Again, ignoring Bill, Ray continues, "For life to be an extension of yourself and a way to be ourselves you must deal with life in the present. To do that, however, means saying *YES* to life. I accept death and all that comes with it. I accept that death is where all parades are headed. I accept that death is the impossibility of all future possibilities. I accept that death takes away all that I ever had and all that I ever will have. But death also plays a crucial role in my awareness of life. It reminds me that existence cannot be postponed. It is through death that I can see what is at stake. Any confrontation with death can lead me to rearrange my priorities. Death is, or can be, wonderful at providing us humans with a greater appreciation of life. But what if death comes before your real life has started as has been the case for many of those I've killed. Now that's tragic."

"Ray, I'm now convinced more than ever that you're one sick fuck."

"Bill, we all have three choices. We either come to accept what is, change what is, or walk away from it. And even in choosing to accept it, you have a choice. You can accept the reality of things for what it is, like not being in denial, and then elect to change it."

"Are you through?"

"No, not yet. Just chew on these three thoughts and you'll see for yourself why you've become the Hunger Artist who dies in oblivion. First, uncertainty, death and impermanence all exist, and we must all learn to co-exist with each of them. You've elected to not only not co-exist with them, but you've denied that they even exist. Two, the measure of your life will be the measure of your courage, contribution, trust, and how much you give back. You've never given anything back. And as a father and husband you never gave anything. Even as a friend, it was always quid pro quo with you. Lastly, if you do not take responsibility for your own predicament, you can never expect to change. And you've never taken responsibility for anything you ever did, and I mean ever."

"Let me ask YOU a question. Do you believe in God?"

"I can't. Not based upon the life I've lived. Because if I believed in God, there is no way I could have lived that life, which for me, was authentic. But I do believe in this. Everything in this world has to be taken as a true reckoning. We love. We hate. We save. We kill. We live. What we do is all there is. What we do is everything. Life like sex is in and out. We suddenly appear out of our mother's womb. We're here and then we're gone. We penetrate, pull out and it's over. And whether it's three minutes of sex or seventy years of life, it's still so damn short. But while we're alive, living, breathing and taking up space, the question that always hangs over us, like the Sword of Damocles is, who the fuck are you?"

"I'm Bill Ott."

"And who in the fuck is Bill Ott? Answer me that."

"You'd make one helluva chess player or one helluva priest."

"Answer the question, Bill."

"You knew going in I couldn't."

"It's sad, really. You're so insecure, so full of self-loathing, you surrounded yourself with people who you thought idolize you so you can feel better about yourself; people never questioned you or your views on the world. You know why?"

"You got the podium. Why?"

"Because they really didn't give any more of a shit about you as you did for them. Like you, all they cared about was themselves and what you could do for them. And now, they REALLY don't care. They want nothing to do with you. Why do you think no one has come to visit you in here?"

"Would you shut up, already?"

"You really are the loneliest man I know, and I can't say I feel sorry for you. "

"So, who's asking you to? And besides, who in the fuck are you? You don't know me for shit. You sit here thinking you're all hot shit because your kid's talking to you. But you know what, you're nothing."

"You ever read Schopenhauer?"

"No. He play for the White Sox?"

"He said, 'It is bad today and everyday will get worse until the worst of all happens.'"

"Now that's uplifting."

"The point is that all of us are sitting on death row and death is THE uncertain certainty that each of us share. Everything is temporary and the worst of all always happens to all of us, eventually. So, the question becomes, what will you do with the time that you have left?"

"All right, Mr. Temporary, I have a question for you."

"Shoot."

"You remember Tick Tock the Croc from Peter Pan?"

"I'll humor you. Yes. The crocodile who ate Captain Hook's arm and swallowed a loud ticking alarm clock."

"That's him."

"Why?"

"Because old Tick Tock the Crock has been following me around and I can't shake him. Worse is that the damn ticking keeps getting louder and louder and keeps me up at night."

"Explain that to me."

"Ray, I've been diagnosed with Pancreatic Cancer. I'm done."

"You tell Devin or Elaine?"

"No. Just you."

"Why?"

"Because I'd rather die as The Hunger Artist than that prize fighter in The Killers."

> "Trails of troubles.
> Roads of battles.
> Paths of victory
> We shall walk."
> Lyrics from Paths of Victory

• CHAPTER TWENTY-NINE •

Exactly eighty-seven days later, the pancreatic cancer won out and the King of White's Tavern was dead. He got his wish and went out like the Hunger Artist and not the prize fighter. Sadly, Bill's son Devin, now a father himself, could never forgive Bill. So, hearing the news of his dad's death, Devin put a match to the picture of he and his dad that he'd been carrying in his wallet for the past twenty-years, and watched it slowly curl in the heat, change color and turn to ash.

As for Ray, he managed to last a little longer and went out the way he wanted to when an unexpected bullet from an assassin's gun finished him off. Apparently, there was an open contract out on him.

Brian King got married and is still living in a small town outside of Birmingham, Alabama.

Donnie Williams got the idea that he'd be ok if he took vitamins while drinking, but he died of cirrhosis of the liver at age 42 anyway.

Davey Joe McLaughlin proved to be a real trooper when he pulled himself out of hospice to attend a White's Tavern/Bowling Alley & Pool Hall reunion. He told me "You know what the doctors told me?" "No, Davey. What?" "They told me I better not drink! And, I told them, what's it gonna do, kill me?!?!" Davey died less than two weeks after that reunion.

Both Ronnie and Bobby Williams are alive and well still living in Chicago, as is Doc Rick Raffin and Macatelli.

One Sorenson died from an overdose and the other is serving a life sentence for stabbing his wife to death. DT also died of an overdose. Elaine became a recluse, still in Chicago, speaking only to her son, who turned out nothing like his father.

None of the mob people mentioned remain and there really isn't much left of the Outfit in Chicago. They've been pretty much replaced by mobs of different cultures, ethnicities and races.

White's Tavern is also long gone. The building remains as a much fancier bar named *Tuckers* specializing in bar food, inexpensive drinks, video poker machines and Blackhawk games. No one, from the owner to the patrons have a clue as to what went on in there when it was White's, but they did tell me that they'd heard it was once a 'wild place'. Nor did they have any knowledge of Tom Tarpey, Chief O'Hallen, Al's Grill or the Triangle Inn.

As Ray Apt so adroitly pointed out, everything comes to an end. Everything is temporary. That both impermanence and finitude are indeed facts of life. But as long as we're here, we attempt to make our mark and leave our mark.

Unfortunately, for most of us, we merely pass on, sometimes before we've ever really lived life, or at least the one we wanted to live, and then 'Bam!', just like that, we're gone and eventually forgotten. Because over time, those people who have kept your picture on the mantel all those years will also someday die and another generation, not knowing any of the people in the picture, will ask, 'Who's that?' and finally toss the picture and the memory of you along with it right in the trash. I have to agree with Ray that death should remind us that existence cannot be postponed, or as Bill brought up that Walt Kelly once wrote, "Don't take life none too serious, cuz it ain't no how permanent."

There is little doubt that the earth will go on for another five billion years, people will come and go, new galaxies will be discovered, certain species will become extinct, man will eventually colonize other planets or other moons, and time will continue to march on. But the one thing that's for sure is that man is but a brief episode in the life of a small planet in a little corner of an extremely large universe. So, do not, under any circumstances, delay life. Find yourself, find your passion, discover who you really are, and live life to the fullest. Yes, life isn't always fair. And yes, some people have a lot more opportunities than others. But it's up to each of us to understand our own individual strengths and gifts and leverage them. First off, you can't learn a damn thing from an experience you're not having. Secondly, each and every one of us has only one shot at life and this ain't no dress rehearsal. Or, in the words of Nietzsche, "You only live once... if then." So, go for it!

THE END

Epilogue

I literally grew up with the majority of the characters mentioned in this book. Bill Ott became my best friend in first grade after we fought to a draw. He and I attended River Grove Grade School where there were some 26 kids in our 8th grade class. I was the class president with Bill being my campaign manager. Of those 26, five of them were sixteen years old and drove to school. One of the funniest memories is when fellow 8th grader, Bob Baus had an argument with Ms. Prost, a third-grade teacher, over a parking space. Another crazy story is when a handful of 8th graders from both River Grove and St. Cyprian's grade schools came up with $100.00 between them in 1963 to put a bet down on me in a chess game to be played at the River Grove Bowling Alley & Pool Hall. My opponent chickened out and proved to be a no show. As you can see, I encountered White's Tavern type characters early on in my life. In high school, I met the notorious Ray Apt my freshman year, as well as many of the other characters in the book. Bill and I never stopped being friends throughout our lives, in spite of our lives being so different.

In high school, Bill was the tough guy, troublemaker, charming comedian, as well as an exceptional athlete lettering in both wrestling and football. Little wonder considering he'd been competing against 16-year-olds since grade school, one of whom was none other than Johnny Bree. In our senior year, I was the class president and a member of several clubs, including the chess club. After high school, I went on to college graduating with a degree. In journalism from Drake University in Des Moines, Iowa in 1971. Other than two or three high school friends, I can't say I was close or stayed in touch with many of the characters in this book. Armed with my degree in Journalism and a low draft number, I sallied forth into the job market only to find one door slamming closed after another. There was a horrible recession going on in 1971 as well as the on-going draft for the war in Viet Nam. As luck would have it, Uncle Sam tapped my draft number and away I went for my physical, which I passed. Two weeks later, I received another letter from Uncle Sam stating they no longer needed my draft number and to have a nice life. With that albatross no longer around my neck, I landed a job as a yard clerk with the Soo Line Railroad in Schiller Park, Illinois. The recession finally broke and I found myself working for Woodall's Publishing in Forest Park, Illinois as an assistant advertising manager. From there, it was back to Des Moines where I landed a job as the State Director of Public Relations for the American National Red Cross in Iowa. All the while, moving on with my life and leaving my friends from grade school and high school behind me. Eventually, I moved back to Chicago and went to work for my dad who was grooming me to take over the family business.

All the while though, in spite of my being back home and taking the train to work, I still wasn't spending much if any time with friends from the area, other than the two or three I'd kept in touch with through college. All of that changed, however, when I went on a movie date in Lombard, Illinois where I heard a female voice whispering from behind me, "Jimmy! Jimmy!!" I finally turned around to see Elaine Stott, also on a date, smiling like a big dog to see me. And I have to say I was just as thrilled to see her, causing both of us to completely ignore our dates. Elaine and I were buds in high school and I was dating her best friend back then. Long story short, she told me I had to go to White's Tavern in River Grove because everybody was there, which I eventually did. And once I did, I never stopped going because not only was she right that everybody WAS there, but the place was a non-stop bizarre circus.

Strange to say that my research for this story began in 1973. Not for a book, but just a collection of one or two-page short vignettes that recorded the more unusual or off the wall antics and events that took place in White's. Back then I was just one of the patrons. As my research progressed, the number of pages grew and I came to realize that not only were many of these people fascinating and unique, but that had it not been for the existence of White's Tavern, this assemblage of people may not have ever happened. Eventually, I brought my entire collection of vignettes into White's and allowed the patrons to read them. It wasn't long before people were seen fighting to read what I'd written and the thirty some pages were being swapped out and traded throughout the bar going from person to person. Funnier still was to see and hear people guffawing in laughter while others exclaimed that they denied ever having done or said something I'd written. In looking back, perhaps much of the credit goes first to Earl then Betty for allowing all the insanity to happen.

So, this story, which began as a collection of moments in time has become the story of a small tavern located in a small Chicago suburb, and the characters that frequented the place. Regarding the two main characters of the book, Bill Ott and Ray Apt, I can safely say people either loved or loathed them. As for Mayor/Chief Tarpey, it was difficult not to like him.

All I can say is that these people made me laugh, experience things I never would have otherwise, were there for me when I needed them, and were damn good friends. I also have to add that work on this book has not only brought me back to River Grove on a number of occasions, but I get together in Las Vegas with several of the characters still living for our Annual River Grove Bowling Alley & Pool Hall Reunion. I truly hope you enjoy the book as much as I did writing it. Thank you.